Everything You Need to Know About the World Series of Poker®—and More!

WORLD SERIES OF POKER
★ OFFICIAL
GUIDEBOOK

D1086752

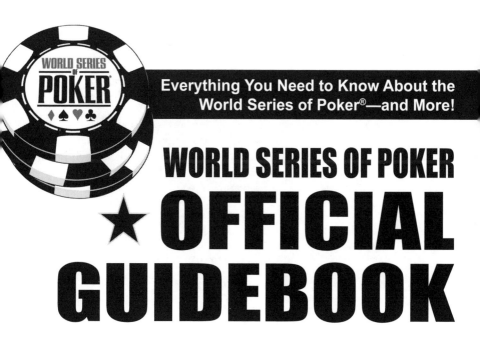

Everything You Need to Know About the World Series of Poker®—and More!

WORLD SERIES OF POKER
★ OFFICIAL
GUIDEBOOK

AVERY CARDOZA & DANA SMITH

CARDOZA PUBLISHING

Cardoza Publishing is the foremost gaming publisher in the world with a library of more than 200 up-to-date and easy-to-read books and strategies. These authoritative works are written by the top experts in their fields and with more than 10,000,000 books in print, represent the most popular gaming books anywhere.

Acknowledgements

We thank the following individuals for their contributions: Seth Palansky, Jack Effel, Daniel Vogel, Elizabeth Anne Hill, and Ty Stewart.

ISBN 10:   1-58042-245-4
ISBN 13: 978-1-58042-245-1
Library of Congress Control Number: 2010926621
Front cover photo of money copyright © Rob Gracie/GreasieWheels.com

Visit our website or write for a full list of products

CARDOZA PUBLISHING

P. O. Box 98115, Las Vegas, NV 89193
Toll-Free Phone (800)577-WINS
email: cardozabooks@aol.com
www.cardozabooks.com

TABLE OF CONTENTS

TABLE OF CONTENTS

CARDOZA PUBLISHING

CARDOZA PUBLISHING

LIST OF CHARTS

INTRODUCTION

by Doyle Brunson
Two-Time World Champion of Poker

1976-77 World Champion of Poker. Author of *Super/System* and *The Godfather of Poker*, Member of Poker Hall of Fame

When I walked into the opening event of the World Series of Poker in 2005, I was mesmerized by what I saw. For the first time since it all began back in 1970, the World Series of Poker had moved from the downtown Horseshoe Casino to the Rio Hotel and Casino just off the Las Vegas Strip. What a change it was! While the Horseshoe was dingy, smoke-filled and cramped, the Rio was massive, airy and wide open. The tournament area at the Rio was 60,000-square-feet, bigger than a football field and equipped with 200 poker tables.

And they needed every one of them.

Some 2,200 players and 500 alternates, players waiting for others to bust out so they could take their seats, swarmed the place. I had never seen anything close to the sheer magnitude of it all. In the Horseshoe, you could easily toss a football from one end of the room to the other. But in the Rio, you'd need an NFL quarterback to reach the far wall and I'm not even sure the best could make that distance. I think you'd need the kicker. The playing area was massive.

Players had been waiting all year for the WSOP to roll around and finally, here it was. During the six-week run, more than 32,000 players would compete in the forty-five events for a prize pool that exceeded $100 million, more than doubling the record set a year earlier. The Main Event itself, the one every player wanted to win, drew more than 5,500 players and had to be spread out over two starting days. Incredibly, all nine players at the Main Event final table would walk away millionaires. That was a far cry from the early days, when the total prize pool for the Main Event would barely tip the scale by today's standards. These developments were something I never could have predicted. I don't think anyone could have.

I couldn't help but remember the humble beginning of the first World Series of Poker elimination tournament in 1971 when six of us sat down to play and Johnny Moss, the winner, walked away with $30,000. What a group it was. Puggy Pearson and the five Texans: Amarillo Slim, Crandell Addington, Jack "Treetop" Straus, Moss and me. As it turns out, all of us ended up in the Poker Hall of Fame.

Nostalgia washed over me. I missed my old friends, the old games at the Horseshoe and those marvelous years. I could see that old gang of road gamblers fighting it out at that first final table. There was also Sailor Roberts, Jimmy Casella, Bill and Ken Smith, Sid Wyman, Benny Binion, "Corky" McCorquodale, Aubrey Day, and all the old-time poker players who are now gone. I wondered what they would say if they could see how far poker had come, if they could see what I was looking at now. It was a strange feeling, an overwhelming one. I felt grateful to be one of the privileged old-timers who got to witness this remarkable evolution of our game.

Standing there in that big room, tears came to my eyes as I looked across the sea of players. Every World Series is a special time of the year for poker players. And for me, it's extra special. I can hardly wait until the cards are in the air.

WELCOME TO THE FABULOUS WORLD SERIES OF POKER

by Avery Cardoza

Which sporting event awards the most money to the champion? Wimbledon, the PGA Masters, the Indianapolis 500? No. The richest sporting event in the world is not played on a grass tennis court, a green golf course or around an asphalt track. Its players compete with clay chips around the green felt tables of the world's most exciting and prestigious poker event of the year—the World Series of Poker.

Not only is the WSOP the field of dreams for poker pros and amateurs alike, it is a field day for millions of fans who gather around their television sets cheering for fearless players who go all out to win by going all-in, risking all their irreplaceable chips in a hotly contested race for the gold bracelet. Young players like 21-year-old Joe Cada who won more than $8 million at the 2009 WSOP championship event. Seasoned champions like Doyle Brunson who has won ten WSOP tournaments over a forty-year poker career. Amateurs like Chris Moneymaker who won $2.5 million in 2003 and let the world know that the playing field of poker is level—you don't have to be a pro to win it!

Whether you're a poker player or a poker fan, there's something special in store for you every year at the WSOP. It may be winning a big prize purse, or the thrill of watching your favorite player teeter on the brink of disaster yet skillfully pull his chips out of the ditch and make it to the final table. Either way, this book gives you the skinny on the inner workings of the fifty or more tournaments played at the WSOP, plus its time honored traditions and history. I think you'll start to feel the sense of belonging and thrill of competition that all poker players—and you fans who enjoy watching them play—share during the WSOP.f

The WSOP offers a wide selection of tournaments designed to give every player a chance to compete in poker's premier spectacular. You can choose from $1,000 to $50,000 buy-ins, limit and no-limit events with high, low or high-low variations, shootouts to freezeouts, and an infinite variety of games—hold'em, Omaha, seven-card stud, lowball, plus multigame tournaments. In these pages, you'll learn strategies for winning at each game, insider tips that will help you play tournament poker or understand it fully when you watch the annual WSOP telecasts on ESPN. You'll also find the storied history of the WSOP, its most treasured moments, and how to enter its great tournaments.

Okay, it's time to get the cards in the air. Let's shuffle up and deal!

THE COLORFUL HISTORY OF THE WORLD SERIES OF POKER

HOW THE WSOP ELEVATED POKER FROM SMOKY BACK ROOMS TO LIVING ROOMS AROUND THE WORLD

by Dana Smith

Long before poker became accepted as a respectable profession, Horseshoe Casino owner Benny Binion and his son Jack firmly believed that poker could be promoted as a competitive sport that players could be proud to play. For decades its domain had been dimly lit, smoky backrooms far removed from mainstream society. Their belief became even stronger after they visited the Reno Holiday Hotel and Casino in 1969. Tom Moore, casino owner, and Vic Vickrey, veteran casino promoter, came up with the idea of a Gaming Fraternity Convention and invited a group of Texas gamblers, along with a few deep-pocket "producers" (losing players with large bankrolls), to attend the loosely organized event. He set up a couple of poker tables in a corner of the casino and "tossed in $3,000 of the hotel's money just so's these fellas would have a little somethin' extra to try shootin' at."

The legendary Doyle Brunson was there: "Moore found out to his dismay that pretty much all we wanted to do was play poker, and he didn't get enough action at his more profitable games, like blackjack and craps. So when Jack Binion asked him if he was holding the convention the next year, Moore figured it wasn't worth the trouble. But Jack and Benny figured it different. When Moore sold his business, they used that tournament as a springboard for what they thought was a grand idea: a World Series of Poker that would be played at their Horseshoe casino in downtown Las Vegas."

Quick to recognize the "convention's" potential, the Binions got a few of their big players together for a social tournament at the Horseshoe in 1970. At the end of the five-game event, the poker players voted Johnny Moss the champion of poker. Thus, the World Series of Poker was launched.

"We had eight players last year, and this year we had thirteen," Benny Binion said in 1973 to Mary Allen Glass in an interview for the Oral History Project at the University of Nevada-Reno. "I look to have better than 20 next year. It's even liable to get up to be 50, might get up to be more than that. It will eventually." Binion's prophecy has come true in spades: The 2008 WSOP at the Rio Hotel and Casino attracted 58,720 entries with 6,844 players in the championship event.

Unlike the spacious Rio with a tournament area the size of several football fields, the entire 1970 event took place in one small room, which later became the baccarat alcove. Binion's Horseshoe did not have a poker room until 1988, when it acquired the Mint, giving the 'Shoe enough space to open its own cardroom. The 63-year-old Johnny Moss, a Texas road gambler, won all the games, receiving a small trophy and all the money he had earned at the table. In a classic photograph taken of the Texas gamblers who attended the event, about 30 men are gathered around a poker table with some trophies sitting on it that they awarded to each other.

"In those days it warn't no one game an' it warn't no freezeout," Moss, who had only an elementary school education, related in an early WSOP brochure written by reporter Al Reinert. "You had to win all the games, win all the money. Then you're the best player, an' they vote on you. I win all five games that year an' they give me a big trophy. In '74 they give me this here gold bracelet with the date engraved on the back. I win a silver cup, too—solid silver, engraved."

In contrast to the neon glitz and advanced technology of modern Las Vegas, Nevada casinos had only seventy licensed poker tables across the entire state in 1970 with forty-seven of them in Clark County. Las Vegas casinos produced $4.5 million of the $5.2 million in revenue the state collected in table rake, that is, less than half the prize money won by the 2008 Main Event Champion.

THE EARLY DAYS AND THE ROAD GAMBLERS

Though today's WSOP is professionally produced and smoothly administered, everything about the first years of the World Series of Poker was amateur except the players—they all were professionals, most of them Texas road gamblers, migrant workers who plied their trade in smoky backrooms nestled along the dusty back roads of the Southern poker circuit. No events were actually scheduled and no one was formally invited, the word simply got around. "If seven 7-card stud players arrived at the Horseshoe at the same time, they'd play the 7-stud contest, provided one of them wasn't asleep," Eric Drache, director of the WSOP in the early days, observed in one of the early WSOP brochures. Most of the road gamblers traveled to the early WSOP mainly to play in the high-stakes side games, as well as enter a tournament or two.

The WSOP format changed in 1971 when the championship was determined by process of elimination. "It was thought that poker had thus far failed to capture press attention because it did not have a series of competitions, as did the other sports, culminating in one grand play-off," a vintage WSOP media guide stated. The buy-in for the newly formatted tournament was $5,000, and this time around, Moss won it by process of elimination. In 1972 the buy-in for the no-limit hold'em championship tournament was increased to $10,000, and a five-card stud tournament was added to the schedule at the players' request.

It wasn't until 1983 when satellites came into existence, that players other than those that traveled the Southern poker circuit or played in the big games in Texas and Louisiana regularly started winning events at the World Series of Poker, beginning with Tom McEvoy, a young accountant from Michigan who won a satellite and went on to win the Main Event that year.

THE WSOP GAINS NATIONAL MEDIA ATTENTION

Amarillo Slim Preston
1972 Main Event Champion
Member of Poker Hall of Fame

Amarillo Slim Preston's victory at the 1972 World Series of Poker triggered an avalanche of national media attention, primarily because the tall toothpick from Texas was a natural-born promoter. With his gift for gab, he went on to make eleven appearances on Johnny Carson's *Tonight Show*, and had three stints on *60 Minutes*. Preston is widely credited with helping build the popularity of the WSOP by bringing poker out of smoky back rooms and into the living rooms of the world.

The first championship event to be videotaped was in 1973. Legendary oddsmaker Jimmy "The Greek" Snyder narrated the colorful commentary for the video, which pictures Jack Binion and Snyder hustling to set up the tables and lay out chips for the thirteen men who had paid to play the Main Event. The players' guests were allowed to sit behind them at the final table. Players could buy insurance on their hands, side bets based on the probability of one hand winning over another. In one hand against Jack "Treetop" Straus, Johnny Moss wanted 2 to 1 insurance, but Binion (who set the odds) offered him only 3 to 2. Moss passed on the wager, but won the hand and knocked Straus out in third place. In the winner-take-all tournament, 45-year-old Walter "Puggy" Pearson won the entire $130,000. Newspapers and magazines printed 7,000 articles about the WSOP that year. The next WSOP videotape came five years later in 1978 when Bobby Baldwin, former Oklahoma road gambler and currently a high-powered CEO in Las Vegas, won the championship.

BACK-TO-BACK MAIN EVENT WINNERS

In 1974, at the age of 67, Johnny Moss became the first three-time winner of the championship event at the WSOP. Stu Ungar repeated Moss' feat twenty-three years later when he won the 1997 Main Event, sixteen years after his repeat wins in 1980-81. Only two other WSOP champions have won back-to-back titles: Doyle Brunson in 1976-77 and Johnny Chan in 1987-88. Coincidentally, both Brunson and Chan almost won three championships each, Brunson when he placed second to Ungar in 1980, and Chan when he was runner-up to Phil Hellmuth Jr. in 1989. Brunson is one of the few poker players to have a two-card hand named for him. He won both Main Events with a 10-2 starting hand, which has become known as a "Doyle Brunson."

The first year for which complete figures for the World Series of Poker were available was in 1977. The prize money of $806,800 was awarded to a total of 366 entrants into the twelve preliminary tournaments and the championship event. The first ladies-only World Series of Poker tournament also was played in 1977. The game was seven-card stud and the victor was awarded $5,580.

THE RISE OF AMATEURS AND SATELLITES

In a shocking upset at the final table of the Main Event in 1979, California advertising executive Hal Fowler defeated well-known Texas professionals Bobby Hoff, Johnny Moss and Crandell Addington to become the first amateur to win the Main Event. The next amateur to win the title was Tom McEvoy in 1983. By the conclusion of the 2008 events, fifteen people who were amateurs at the time they played the tournament—student, farmer, attorney, chiropractor, business owner—have won the WSOP Main Event. McEvoy also made WSOP history as the first player to win his seat in the Main Event via a satellite, and has continued his tournament career through the years, winning the Champion of Champions crown in 2009 by defeating nineteen other world champions of poker. Today, satellite tournaments are a primary portal into the WSOP preliminary tournaments and the Main Event.

Tom McEvoy
1983 Main Event Champion
2009 Champion of Champions

The championship tournament drew more than 100 entrants for the first time in 1982, when Jack Straus defeated 104 players for $520,000. Straus became the poster boy of the poker axiom, "All it takes is a chip and a chair," as he had only one chip left midway through the final-table action and built it into the winning stack, making his triumph all the more spectacular. By 2006, the number of entrants in the Main Event had escalated to a record 8,773 when talent agent Jamie Gold won the title and $12 million.

Marking another WSOP milestone, the 1990 Main Event Champion, Mansour Matloubi from Wales, became the first citizen of a country other than the United States to win the Main Event. Since then, the World Series of Poker has become an international happening. In 2008, players from 124 nations participated in WSOP tournaments, including twenty-two-year-old main-event winner, Peter Eastgate from Denmark, who held the record for the youngest player ever to win the title until 2009 when twenty-one year old Joe Cada claimed that crown.

STU UNGAR WINS THIRD TITLE IN 1997

It was a scorcher on Fremont Street in Las Vegas by the time Stu Ungar and John Strzemp got heads-up for the championship duel on the outdoor stage at the 1997 WSOP. Gabe Kaplan sat in the commentator's box with ESPN cameramen toting equipment the size of Mac trucks that emitted enough heat to cancel out the steam misters carefully installed underneath the poker table for the players' comfort.

Although the spectators and we members of the press who were crowded into the sweaty bleachers enjoyed the thrill of watching Ungar's return to the arena after his seventeen-year hiatus from poker, mercifully, the duel in the sun ended after only six hands. Ungar raised before the flop with A-4 and Strzemp called with A-8. The A-5-3 flop maintained Strzemp's lead, but it also gave Ungar a gutshot straight draw. When

Strzemp bet, Ungar moved all in and the casino executive pushed his last chips to the middle. Ungar won his third championship title when a deuce fell on the river to complete his ace-to-5 straight.

This dramatic finish was not the first time that Ungar had won the title by making a gutshot wheel on the final hand. In 1980, the brash, young rookie played heads-up with the legendary Doyle Brunson and hit a wheel card on fourth street to break Brunson, depriving the "Godfather of Poker" of his third championship title in a near photo finish.

Regarded as perhaps the greatest tournament player in the history of poker, Ungar used his uncanny reading ability and perfectly timed moves to carve his name into WSOP history and legend when he made an unparalleled comeback from near obscurity to win the title on a steamy spring day in 1997. It was the last time most people ever saw him play. A year later, The Comeback Kid died at the age of forty-five, a victim of his vices.

JOHNNY CHAN AND ERIK SEIDEL MATCH WITS IN 1988

Johnny Chan
1987-88 Main Event Champion
Member of Poker Hall of Fame

The 1988 championship event is a classic in World Series of Poker history, in part because Johnny Chan won it for the second consecutive year, but primarily because the final hand he played against runner-up Erik Seidel was featured in the 1998 movie, *Rounders*, starring Matt Damon as a frustrated college student who travels to Las Vegas to play in the "biggest game in town."

When the final hand began, defending World Champion Chan had $1,374,000 in chips and challenger Seidel had only $296,000. They both entered the pot for the minimum bet. The flop gave Chan the nut straight and Seidel a pair of queens. Chan bet a modest $40,000. Not suspecting a trap and playing beyond his experience to get this far in the tournament, newcomer Seidel raised $50,000 with top pair. The crafty Chan flat-called. The turn card was an innocuous deuce and Chan checked his unbeatable hand. Deceived by Chan's underbet on the flop and his check on the turn, Seidel pushed in all of his remaining chips. The impotent river card changed nothing, and Chan won the championship of poker for the second year in a row.

Now a respected poker professional who has won eight WSOP gold bracelets, Seidel gave me his take on his intriguing 1988 match with Chan. "It was surreal to find myself heads-up with Johnny at the final table. I was pretty bad in those days, especially shorthanded," he said. "I remember looking at the whole scene, the lights and cameras and all those chips, and thinking, 'What in the world am I doing here, playing heads-up for the world championship?' It was pretty awful to be in such a great spot and to be so unprepared for it. Still, it was the most incredible experience—to play for four days and get heads-up with Chan—just knowing that I could do it, that I could play at that level."

Matt Damon and Ed Norton, the stars of *Rounders*, actually played in the 1998 WSOP to promote their movie. When an *Entertainment Tonight* reporter asked the pair how they fit in with Doyle and Slim and "some of these old characters," Damon answered, "I don't know that we did." Norton added, "We're skinnier than most of them."

MONEYMAKER IGNITES POKER EXPLOSION IN 2003

Playing in the biggest Main Event field to that date, accountant and amateur poker player Chris Moneymaker defeated 838 competitors in 2003 to win the WSOP Main Event. An overnight celebrity, Moneymaker quickly made the rounds of the talk shows, including David Letterman, and his intriguing rags-to-riches story appeared in major print media around the world. Thousands of casual players regarded his victory as proof that if an amateur like Moneymaker could make $2.5 million playing poker, so could they.

Chris Moneymaker
2003 Main Event Champion

The unassuming and personable Moneymaker is widely credited with providing the spark that led to the rebirth of poker at walk-in casinos and the vast popularity of televised poker events.

HARRAH'S ASSUMES OWNERSHIP OF THE WSOP IN 2004

Harrah's Entertainment acquired the World Series of Poker in 2004. From 1970 until 1998, Jack Binion and his father Benny had run the show at the Horseshoe on Fremont Street. In 1999, Becky Binion Behnen acquired ownership of the legendary casino and its world-famous tournament in a family financial arrangement. Falling upon hard times in her efforts to keep pace with the modern casino industry, the Binion heiress sold the Horseshoe and the WSOP.

Since Harrah's Entertainment has assumed ownership of the WSOP, the tournament has grown significantly each year, from 13,036 total player registrations for all tournament events in 2004, to 58,720 in 2008. That year, the WSOP awarded $180,774,427 in prize money. According to a December 2007 article in *The Economist*, poker is the third most watched sport on cable television, following the NFL and NASCAR. The WSOP also has expanded its tournaments internationally with the guidance and professional leadership of Harrah's Entertainment. The first-ever WSOP event held outside the U.S. took place in September 2007 in London at the Casino at the Empire in Leicester Square.

THE BATTLE OF THE BRACELETS

No sporting event would be as compelling without its rivalries, its hotly contested races to the finish line, its contests of strength against cunning.

WSOP Media Director Nolan Dalla captured the drama and allure of the WSOP when he wrote, "What happened at 3:18 am on a Sunday night in 2005 during the $2,500 pot-limit hold'em event ranks right up there as one of the game's greatest moments. That's when Johnny Chan won a record tenth WSOP gold bracelet after a two-year epoch during which poker's three most famous players—Doyle Brunson, Phil Hellmuth and Chan—had been locked in a virtual dead heat with nine gold bracelets each. It would be hard to decide which was more exciting—the final duel between Chan and Phil Laak—or the fanfare of media and fans swarming around Chan afterwards."

The dramatic turn of events occurred when Chan was dealt Q-Q and his opponent was dealt A-A. The 1988-89 world champion was all in, as well as being in jeopardy of losing everything when a queen showed up on the flop to win the pot for him and put him in the chip lead—and the bracelet lead over second-place contender Doyle Brunson.

Chan's lead in the battle for the bracelets lasted less than a week. In Dalla's account, "Four remarkable days after Johnny Chan won his tenth WSOP title, Doyle Brunson returned to poker's center stage. In front of an SRO crowd and a barrage of ESPN television cameras, Brunson rewrote the record books one more time when he won his tenth gold bracelet." His tying win came in the $5,000 six-handed no-limit hold'em tournament.

Brunson recorded this victory in *My 50 Most Memorable Hands*, the title of his 2007 book, written almost thirty years after his landmark *Super/System*. "Johnny Chan, Phil Hellmuth, and I had nine bracelets each and everyone was watching us closely in 2005. Then Chan won a no-limit hold'em tournament and got his tenth. Phil and I both congratulated him and we both resolved in our heart to catch him.

"A few days later I found myself at the last table with just Minh Ly and myself left. I had a pretty nice lead on him but the antes and blinds had gotten so big your chips could literally evaporate. So when Minh had the button and didn't raise, I had a strong feeling he was weak. I moved in on him, and to my surprise he called and turned over K-Q. 'What you have, 10-2?' he asked. 'No, I've got his big brother,' I laughed."

Ly was referring to the surprisingly similar 10-2 hands with which Brunson won back-to-back championship titles in 1976-77. This time Doyle had a 10-3. Amazingly, a 3 came on the flop to give Brunson the win and tie him with Chan in the bracelet race.

As the gold bracelet was fastened to the 73 year-old champion's wrist, a reporter asked how it felt to still be able to compete at poker's highest level. "It's hard to substitute for experience," Brunson said. "No one has more poker experience than I do. Then again, no one here is as old as I am."

And certainly not the man who broke the 10-bracelet deadlock, a player who is one of only three people to win three gold bracelets at the WSOP within a single year—Phil Hellmuth Jr.

Coming into the 2006 WSOP, Hellmuth lagged one bracelet win behind Brunson and Chan. In one of the final tournaments preceding the Main Event, he finally broke the barrier that had separated him from winning membership into the exclusive "Ten Win" Club. His coveted victory came in

Phil Hellmuth, Jr.
1989 Main Event Champion
Member of Poker Hall of Fame

the $1,000 no-limit hold'em with rebuys event against a field of 754 players who made 1,691 rebuys. In his sixth cash and third final-table appearance of 2006, the volatile Hellmuth was at the epicenter of an enthusiastic crowd of fans chanting "Ten! Ten! Ten!"

And with that, the three-way race to win gold bracelet number eleven was on.

It was short. And it was very sweet for Hellmuth, who won the $1,500 no-limit hold'em event the next year in 2007 to become the first and only member of the "Heavenly Eleven" Club. Not only did Hellmuth win his record eleventh bracelet, he won it against the largest field he had ever conquered, 2,628 entries, in his 38th WSOP final-table appearance.

"I honestly would have paid a million dollars for this moment," Hellmuth told a cheering crowd afterward. "I'm maybe the best hold'em player in the world, at the top of my game, and I felt it would be a shame if I didn't win the bracelet." As the crowd faded and he walked away from the staging area, Hellmuth whispered one final question to the tournament director. "So, how much money did I win?"

And that just seems to be the way it is at the World Series of Poker. First the bracelet, then the money.

WORLD SERIES OF POKER LEGENDARY MILESTONES

The colorful history of the World Series of Poker has been punctuated with photo-finish duels for the championship, colorful players from all walks of life, and exciting races to win the most gold bracelets, along with the pomp and circumstance of the annual induction ceremony of the WSOP Hall of Fame. This section gives you the cast of characters in the continuing drama on the world's most famous poker theater.

THE WSOP HALL OF FAME

The highest honor a poker player can be awarded is being inducted into the prestigious WSOP Hall of Fame. Seven players were inducted into the inaugural Hall of Fame in 1979, including three-time champion of poker, Johnny Moss. Since that time, only one or two people have achieved poker's highest honor each year. Following is the complete list of members and the year they were inducted.

MEMBERS OF THE HALL OF FAME

1979

Johnny Moss won the World Championship of Poker three times (1970-71, 1974) and is often called the "grand old man of poker." A former Texas road gambler, Moss defeated Nick "The Greek" Dandolos in a marathon poker game at Binion's Horseshoe in 1949, which is credited with being the forerunner of the WSOP.

Mike Sexton
Member of Poker Hall of Fame

Nick "The Greek" Dandolos was known for making astronomical wagers in Las Vegas casinos. Late in life, almost destitute, Dandolos played low-limit poker in Southern California. Asked how he could bet millions of dollars once and now play for $5 chips, he was purported to have said "Hey, it's action."

Felton "Corky" McCorquodale was a famous high-stakes gambler in the early days. He helped introduce a new poker game, Texas hold 'em, to Las Vegas casinos in 1963.

Red Winn, another high-stakes gambler from the early days of poker, played all poker games well.

Sid Wyman, a noted gambler who excelled at poker, co-owned several Vegas casinos from the 1950s to the 1970's, including the Sands, Riviera, and Dunes. The Dunes halted casino play for two minutes at the hour of his funeral.

James Butler "Wild Bill" Hickok, was a 19th century gambler, lawman and sharpshooter who died holding aces and eights, the famous "Dead Man's Hand," during a poker game in Deadwood when he was shot in the back by "Crooked Nose" McCall.

Edmond Hoyle was a 17th century British author who wrote rules books for games that were used to settle difference during games. The phrase "according to Hoyle" has become synonymous with abiding by the rules.

1980

T. "Blondie" Forbes, a vintage road gambler on the old Southern circuit, played no-limit hold'em with all the best poker players in the early days of Las Vegas.

1981

Bill Boyd was one of the best five-card stud players in the world, and won the 5-Card Stud championship at the WSOP. He was ceremonially dealt the first poker hands at both the Golden Nugget and Mirage cardrooms.

1982

Tom Abdo was a consummate gambler in the early era of poker. After suffering a heart attack at the poker table, Tom turned to another player and asked him to count his chips down and save his seat. He died that night, intending to return to the game.

1983

Joe Bernstein was one of the original Texas road gamblers who moved to Las Vegas after hold'em was introduced. He was known not only for playing the highest stakes poker games, but also for dressing stylishly at the poker table.

1984

Murph Harrold was widely regarded as one of the best deuce-to-seven draw (Kansas City lowball) players of all time.

1985

Red Hodges was famous among early poker players for being one of the best seven-card stud players in history.

1986

Henry Green, a road gambler from Alabama who was skilled at all poker games, was widely known for his implacable composure under pressure at the table.

1987

Walter Clyde "Puggy" Pearson, the 1973 World Champion of Poker, was a colorful figure in the early days of the WSOP. The cigar-chomping Tennessee gambler was a great seven-card stud player noted for his aggressive style and homespun philosophy.

1988

Doyle Brunson, the 1976-1977 World Champion of Poker, was the first player to win $1 million in tournament play. His book *Super/System* is probably the best-selling poker strategy book ever written. Often referred to as "The Godfather of Poker," Brunson has won 10 gold bracelets at the WSOP, becoming a living legend of poker.

Jack Straus, the 1982 World Champion of Poker, was a Texas road gambler known for his aggressive and imaginative play. Nicknamed "Treetop," Straus stood six-foot-six inches tall. He died in 1988 after suffering a heart attack during a high-stakes poker game at the Bicycle Club in California.

1989

Fred "Sarge" Ferris, the son of Lebanese immigrants, became a professional gambler to escape the poverty of his youth, going on to win the 2-7 draw poker title at the 1980 WSOP. In 1983, the Internal Revenue Service seized $46,000 worth of chips from Ferris during a high-stakes game at the Horseshoe.

1990

Benny Binion founded the Horseshoe Casino in Las Vegas, where he inaugurated the World Series of Poker as a gamblers convention in 1970. The colorful cowboy and astute businessman from Texas is reputed to have arrived in Las Vegas in the 1950s with the trunk of his car filled with cash. He died on Christmas Day 1989, at age 85.

1991

David Edward "Chip" Reese came to Las Vegas in 1974 with $400 in his pocket and started playing poker at the $10 limit tables, quickly becoming one of the game's best all-around high-stakes players. At age 40, the Dartmouth graduate was the youngest player ever inducted into the Poker Hall of Fame. After winning the inaugural $50,000 buy-in H.O.R.S.E. tournament at the 2006 WSOP, the event was named in his honor. Chip Reese died in 2007, at age 56.

1992

Thomas Austin "Amarillo Slim" Preston, the 1972 World Champion of Poker, is widely credited with "legitimizing" poker as a "respectable" sport through his appearances on nationally broadcast talk shows in the 1970s. The Texas gambler, rancher, and tournament promoter also is known for his colorful poker yarns.

1993

Jack "Gentleman Jack" Keller, the 1984 World Champion of Poker, was one of the most consistent poker players at the WSOP in the 1980s, and was recognized as a formidable tournament competitor.

1996

Julius Oral "Little Man" Popwell was a gambler of near-mythical stature who played poker with Johnny Moss and other old-time Texas road gamblers in the 1940s and '50s.

1997

Roger Moore entered his first World Series of Poker in 1974. Born into adversity as the son of a sharecropper, Moore became one of poker's most determined and formidable players. He won the $5,000 buy-in 7-Card Stud championship at the 1994 WSOP.

2001

Stu "The Kid" Ungar was one of the greatest no-limit poker players in history. He won back-to-back Main Events in 1980-81 before the age of 26, and ten major no-limit hold'em championships with $5,000 or higher buy-ins. In 1997, Ungar won his record third Mian Event Championship.

2002

Lyle Berman prefers playing high-stakes cash games to tournaments, although he has won three titles at the World Series of Poker (limit Omaha in 1989, no-limit hold'em in 1992, and 2-7 draw in 1994). Berman, an astute businessman, has gained international fame as the co-founder of the World Poker Tour.

Johnny Chan won back-to-back Main Events in 1987 and 1988, and currently has won 10 bracelets at the WSOP. Chan gained international fame when his duel with Erik Seidel at the final table in 1988 was shown in the movie, *Rounders*, in which he was featured as star Matt Damon's idol. Known as one of the finest no-limit hold'em players in the world, Chan's nickname is "The Orient Express."

2003

Bobby Baldwin, the 1978 World Champion of Poker, was known in the early days as "The Owl" because of his uncanny ability to read the cards of his opponents in road games across Oklahoma and Texas. After aligning his business skills with those of Steve Wynn in the 1980s, Baldwin has since gone on to become one of the best-known casino CEOs on the Las Vegas strip.

2004

Berry Johnston, the 1986 World Series of Poker champion, is well known for his unflappable composure at the poker table. He has consistently cashed at the WSOP since 1982, and was the player with the most all-time cashes in 2004.

2005

Jack Binion hosted the first World Series of Poker in 1970. For over 50 years, his innovations and style have led to great success in the casino industry. Inheriting the Horseshoe legacy from his father, Benny Binion, Jack developed the downtown casino into a Las Vegas icon renowned for its high limits and generous odds.

Crandell Addington is a world-famous poker ambassador who has enjoyed an extremely successful career playing high-stakes poker, pitting his skills against the game's biggest names. He is the author of "The History of No-Limit Texas Hold'em," a colorful chapter in Doyle Brunson's book, *Super System 2*.

2006

T.J. Cloutier, who has won six gold bracelets, has placed four times among the top five at the final table of the Main Event at the World Series of Poker, including two second-place finishes in 1985 and 2000. The author of five poker strategy books, Cloutier is the only person in WSOP history to win tournaments in all three types of Omaha.

Bill Baxter, widely known as arguably the best lowball poker player of all time, has won seven gold bracelets in World Series of Poker lowball tournaments, and is sixth on the all-time bracelet wins chart. He also is well known for staking champion Stu Ungar in his comeback Main Event win in 1997.

2007

Phillip J. Hellmuth, Jr., the 1989 World Champion of Poker, holds a record 11 World Series of Poker bracelets. Nicknamed "Poker Brat" for his sometimes erratic behavior at televised poker events, Hellmuth holds the records for most WSOP cashes and is eighth on the all-time money list. He is the author of several poker books and DVD programs.

Barbara Enright is the only woman to make the final table of the World Series of Poker Main Event, finishing in 5th place in 1995. A two-time Ladies World Champion of Poker, Enright was the first woman to win an open event at the WSOP, a pot-limit hold'em tournament in 1996. She was an inaugural inductee into the Women in Poker Hall of Fame in 2007.

2008

Duane "Dewey" Tomko, a former kindergarten teacher and golf course owner, has won three gold bracelets. He began playing poker for profit as a teenager, thus financing his college degree. He has played every WSOP Main Event since 1974, finishing second to champion Carlos Mortenson in 2001, as well as second to Jack Straus in 1982.

Henry Orenstein holds more than 100 patents, including U.S. Patent 5,451,054 which gave him the exclusive right in the United States to detect and display hole cards in poker games, one of the principal reasons for the popularity of televised poker events. Widely credited with helping spur the growth of poker, the Holocaust survivor has played a prominent role in televised poker programming.

2009

Mike Sexton, the popular TV commentator for the World Poker Tour, has long been a mover and shaker in the annals of poker. He has cashed forty-five times at the WSOP and has won one gold bracelet. Sexton co-founded the Tournament of Champions of Poker, a milestone in poker history. A U.S.

Air Force veteran, he graduated from college on a gymnastics scholarship and later became a dance instructor before turning to professional poker in 1977.

THE POKER HALL OF FAME	
1979	Nick "The Greek" Dandolos James Butler "Wild Bill Hickok" Edmond Hoyle Felton "Corky" McCorquodale Johnny Moss Red Winn Sid Wyman
1980	T "Blondie" Forbes
1981	Bill Boyd
1982	Tom Abdo
1983	Joe Bernstein
1984	Murph Harrold
1985	Red Hodges
1986	Henry Green
1987	Walter Clyde "Puggy" Pearson
1988	Doyle Brunson/Jack Straus
1989	Fed "Sarge" Ferris
1990	Benny Binion
1991	David "Chip" Reese
1992	Thomas Austin "Amarillo Slim" Preston
1993	Jack Keller
1996	Julius Oral "Little Man" Popwell
1997	Roger Moore

(continued)

THE POKER HALL OF FAME	
2001	Stu "The Kid" Ungar
2002	Lyle Berman/Johnny Chan
2003	Bobby Baldwin
2004	Berry Johnston
2005	Crandall Addington/Jack Binion
2006	Billy Baxter/T.J. Cloutier
2007	Barbara Enright/Phil Hellmuth Jr.
2008	Henry Orenstein/Duane "Dewey" Tomko
2009	Mike Sexton

TEN LEGENDARY MILESTONES AT THE WSOP

	TEN LEGENDARY MOMENTS AT THE WSOP
1.	Six players buy a $5,000 entry into the first WSOP elimination tournament in 1971 with champion Johnny Moss winning the entire $30,000 purse.
2.	Upon winning the championship in 1972, the flamboyant Amarillo Slim Preston appears on Johnny Carson's *Tonight Show* and *60 Minutes* to bring global respectability to poker by advancing the game from smoky backrooms into living rooms around the world.
3.	In 1977, Doyle Brunson wins his second consecutive Main Event holding the same card ranks, a 10 and a deuce, to become the first world champion of poker to have a hand named in his honor.
4.	In 1983 Tom McEvoy becomes the first satellite winner to win the Main Event in a classic seven-hour heads-up match against runner-up Rod Peate, also a satellite winner.
5.	The heads-up battle between winner Johnny Chan and runner-up Erik Seidel in the 1988 championship event is featured in the 1998 movie, *Rounders*, starring Matt Damon as a college student who travels to Las Vegas to play in the WSOP.
6.	In a field of 312 players, Stu Ungar wins his third championship in 1997 for a $1 million payday.
7	Amateur Chris Moneymaker wins the championship for $2.5 million in 2003 in a field of 839 players, sparking worldwide interest in live poker tournaments..
8.	Doyle Brunson wins his tenth WSOP gold bracelet in 2005, 28 years after winning back-to-back world championships in 1976-77.
9.	A record-breaking 8,773 players enter the 2006 $10,000 Main Event, with champion Jamie Gold receiving a record $12 million for his win.
10.	Professional player Phil Hellmuth Jr. wins his eleventh gold bracelet in 2007, edging out Johnny Chan and Doyle Brunson for top spot on the bracelet ladder.

WINNERS OF THE MAIN EVENT

From 1970 to 2009, the WSOP has crowned a total of thirty-four Main Event Champions. Johnny Moss was elected champion in 1970 and won the championship in competition twice. Stu Ungar won the championship three times, and Doyle Brunson and Johnny Chan have won it twice. All four of these champions won titles in back-to-back years.

Dan Harrington
1995 Main Event Champion
Author of *Harrington on Hold'em*

Seven of the thirty-four Main Event champions—Johnny Moss, Puggy Pearson, Stu Ungar, Hal Fowler, Jack Straus, Jack Keller and Bill Smith—have since passed, leaving twenty-seven living players able to go for a repeat championship title. Following is a list of the Main Event winners and their spoils of victory.

WSOP MAIN EVENT WINNERS			
YEAR	WINNER	ENTRANTS	PRIZE
1970	Johnny Moss	7	Silver Cup
1971	Johnny Moss	6	$30,000
1972	Thomas "Amarillo Slim" Preston	8	$80,000
1973	Walter "Puggy" Pearson	13	$130,000
1974	Johnny Moss	16	$160,000
1975	Brian "Sailor" Roberts	21	$210,000
1976	Doyle Brunson	22	$220,000
1977	Doyle Brunson	34	$340,000
1978	Bobby Baldwin	42	$210,000
1979	Hal Fowler	54	$270,000
1980	Stu Ungar	73	$385,000
1981	Stu Ungar	75	$375,000

WSOP LEGENDARY MILESTONES

WSOP MAIN EVENT WINNERS			
YEAR	WINNER	ENTRANTS	PRIZE
1982	Jack "Treetop" Strauss	104	$520,000
1983	Tom McEvoy	108	$540,000
1984	Jack Keller	132	$660,000
1985	Bill Smith	140	$700,000
1986	Berry Johnston	141	$570,000
1987	Johnny Chan	152	$625,000
1988	Johnny Chan	167	$700,000
1989	Phil Hellmuth Jr.	178	$755,000
1990	Mansour Matloubi	194	$895,000
1991	Brad Dougherty	215	$1,000,000
1992	Hamid Datsmalchi	201	$1,000,000
1993	Jim Bechtel	220	$1,000,000
1994	Russ Hamilton	268	$1,000,000
1995	Dan Harrington	273	$1,000,000
1996	Huck Seed	295	$1,000,000
1997	Stu Ungar	312	$1,000,000
1998	Scotty Nguyen	350	$1,000,000
1999	Noel Furlong	393	$1,000,000
2000	Chris "Jesus" Ferguson	512	$1,500,000
2001	Carlos Mortensen	613	$1,500,000
2002	Robert Varkonyi	631	$2,000,000
2003	Chris Moneymaker	839	$2,500,000
2004	Grey Raymer	2,576	$5,000,000
2005	Joe Hachem	5,619	$7,500,000
2006	Jamie Gold	8,773	$12,000,000
2007	Jerry Yang	6,358	$8,250,000
2008	Peter Eastgate	6,844	$9,152,416
2009	Joe Cada	6,494	$8,547,042

LEADING MONEY WINNERS AT THE WSOP

Greg Raymer
2004 World Champion of Poker

WSOP MONEY LEADERS 1970-2009		
POSITION	PLAYER	AMOUNT
1st	Jamie Gold	$12,057,518
2nd	Peter Eastgate	$9,221.395
3rd	Joe Cada	$8,574,649
4th	Jerry Yang	$8,250,000
5th	Joseph Hachem	$7,982,111
6th	Allen Cunningham	$6,714,388
7th	Greg Raymer	$6,487,512
8th	Ivan Demidov	$6,388,017
9th	Paul Wasicka	$6,217,738
10th	Phil Hellmuth	$6,105,254
11th	Darvin Moon	$5,182,601
12th	Phil Ivey	$4,861,490
13th	Michael Binger	$4,853,748
14th	Tuan Lam	$4,851,424
15th	Scotty Nguyen	$4, 727,717
16th	Dennis Phillips	$4,699,375
17th	T.J. Cloutier	$4,324,186
18th	David Williams	$4,299,996

WSOP LEGENDARY MILESTONES

POSITION	PLAYER	AMOUNT
WSOP MONEY LEADERS 1970-2009		
19th	Steve Dannenmann	$4,271,489
20th	Johnny Chan	$4,241,448
21st	Erik Seidel	$4,220,577
22nd	Chris Ferguson	$4,027,077
23rd	Ylon Schwartz	$4,021,303
24th	Antoine Saout	$3,662,250
25th	Dan Harrington	$3,524,476
26th	Freddy Deeb	$3,453,659
27th	Josh Arieh	$3,411,511
28th	Vitaly Lunkin	$3,378,286
29th	Daniel Negreanu	$3,309,349
30th	Rhett Butler	$3,221,237
31st	Scott Montgomery	$3,177,030
32nd	John Juanda	$3, 159,726
33rd	Mike Matusow	$3,114,600
34th	Raymond Rahme	$3,063,786
35th	Doyle Brunson	$2.944,053
36th	Eric Buchman	$2,823,680
37th	Richard Lee	$2,822,827
38th	Huck Seed	$2,805,737
39th	Dewey Tomko	$2,637,620
40th	John Barch	$2,589,869
41st	David Chiu	$2,575,481
42nd	Jeffrey Lisandro	$2,575,321
43rd	Chris Moneymaker	$2,532,041
44th	Darus Suharto	$2,449,269
45th	Erik Friberg	$2,430,371
46th	Doug Kim	$2,406,181
47th	Layne Flack	$2,318,537
48th	Aaron Kanter	$2,314,886
49th	Alexander Kravchenko	$2,312,413
50th	Barry Greenstein	$2,259,097

PLAYERS WHO HAVE WON THE MOST GOLD BRACELETS

Erik Seidel
Winner of Eight WSOP
Gold Bracelets

POSITION	PLAYER	# OF BRACELETS
WSOP BRACELET LEADER LIST		
1970-2009		
1st	Phil Hellmuth Jr.	11
2nd	Doyle Brunson	10
	Johnny Chan	10
4th	Johnny Moss	9
5th	Erik Seidel	8
6th	Phil Ivey	7
	Billy Baxter	7
8th	Layne Flack	6
	Men "the Master" Nguyen	6
	Jay Heimowitz	6
	T.J. Cloutier	6

WSOP LEGENDARY MILESTONES

WSOP BRACELET LEADER LIST 1970-2009		
POSITION	PLAYER	# OF BRACELETS
12th	Scotty Nguyen	5
	Allen Cunningham	5
	Ted Forrest	5
	Chris "Jesus" Ferguson	5
	Berry Johnston	5
	Gary "Bones" Berland	5
	Stu "The Kid" Ungar	5
20th	John Juanda	4
	Daniel Negreanu	4
	David Chiu	4
	Huck Seed	4
	Mickey Appelman	4
	Artie Cobb	4
	Tom McEvoy	4
	Lakewood Louie	4
	Thomas "Amarillo Slim" Preston	4
	Walter "Puggy" Pearson	4
	Jeffrey Lisandro	4

THE PLAYERS WHO HAVE MADE THE MOST CASHES AT THE WSOP

T.J. Cloutier
Member of Poker Hall of Fame.
Has won six WSOP bracelets.

WSOP ALL-TIME CASHES 1970-2009		
POSITION	PLAYER	# OF CASHES
1st	Phil Hellmuth Jr.	75
2nd	Men Nguyen	65
3rd	Chris Ferguson	60
4th	Berry Johnston	57
	Erik Seidel	57
6th	T.J.Cloutier	55
	Humberto Brenes	55
8th	Chau Giang	51
9th	John Juanda	50
	Chris Bjorn	50
11th	David Chiu	48
12th	John Cernuto	47
	Brent Carter	46
13th	Thor Hansen	46
	Mike Sexton	46

POSITION	PLAYER	# OF CASHES
WSOP ALL-TIME CASHES **1970-2009**		
16th	Barry Greenstein	44
17h	Howard Lederer	43
	Daniel Negreanu	43
	An Tran	43
20th	Johnny Chan	42
	Anthony Cousineau	42
	Dewey Tomko	42
23rd	Allen Cunningham	41
24th	Mickey Appleman	39
25th	Ken Flaton	38
	Steve Zolotow	38
27th	Annie Duke	37
	Tom McEvoy	37
	Scotty Nguyen	37
	Huck Seed	37
31st	Dan Heimiller	36
	Jay Heimowitz	36
	Phil Ivey	36
	Mel Judah	36
35th	Frank Henderson	35

PLAYERS OF THE YEAR

In 2004 the WSOP began awarding Player of the Year honors for best performance in the WSOP series of tournaments. Daniel Negreanu, the first WSOP Player of the Year, also won Card Player magazine's Poker Player of the Year award in 2004. Interestingly, none of the POY winners to date have won the Main Event.

Daniel Negreanu
2004 Player of the Year.
Author of *Power Hold'em Strategy*

PLAYERS OF THE YEAR				
YEAR	WINNER	BRACELETS	FINAL TABLES	MONEY FINISHES
2004	Daniel Negreanu	1	5	6
2005	Allen Cunningham	1	4	5
2006	Jeff Madsen	2	4	4
2007	Tom Schneider	2	3	3
2008	Erick Lindgren	1	3	5
2009	Jeffrey Lisandro	3	4	6

 # PLAYING IN THE WSOP

You've made the big decision. You're ready to put your chips on the table and your heart in the game. But hold on—you can't win it if you're not officially in it. Here's the scoop on how to register to play in a tournament at the WSOP.

REGISTERING FOR TOURNAMENTS

In popular tournaments, particularly the lower buy-in no-limit hold'em events, long lines form hours before the tournament is scheduled to begin. If you want to avoid the hassles of a tournament that attracts *thousands* of players, be sure to register in advance.

Capacity is limited and entry is on a first come, first serve basis. Once an event's maximum enrollment is reached or the expected table capacity is filled, the event will be declared a sellout. World Series of Poker officials report that no event has ever sold out up to the day before the event; however, sellouts often happen on the day of the event. No alternates are seated at the World Series of Poker, so tournament officials strongly encourage you to pre-register to guarantee your seat. Note that you cannot play if you're under the age of twenty-one as it is prohibited by the State of Nevada.

You have two ways to register for WSOP events: you can begin the process online at WSOP.com or register in person at the main cage of the Rio at least two weeks in advance, or at the WSOP tournament area itself. Let's look at both.

How to Pre-Register Online

You can begin the pre-registration process online at www.worldseriesofpoker.com. Go to the "Event Registration" tab for full details on how to pre-register up to two weeks prior to the start of the event you want to play. The deposit required is the full amount of the event's entry fee. You must finalize your registration in person at the Will Call desk in the Rio by presenting proof of identity and your Total Rewards card. If you decide to play an event other than what you originally selected during pre-registration, you can apply your deposit to a new event at this time.

Additional pre-registration instructions and registration forms for each individual event are available on the WSOP website at http://www.worldseriesofpoker.com/registration/.

REGISTRATION CHECKLIST

- Bring your ID
- Bring your Total Rewards card
- Bring payment or proof of payment

How to Register During the World Series of Poker

If you plan to register once you get to Las Vegas, you can register in person when you arrive in town at the WSOP cage in the Amazon Room, or before that time at the main casino cage. The WSOP cage is open 24/7, but you'll find lines much shorter after 7 p.m. Waiting until the day of your event to register is ill-advised, but if you must do so, get to the Rio as early as possible. Lines form early and might cause you to be late for your event. Be sure to bring your ID and Total Rewards card. You can only register yourself for events. You cannot register other players. Only players whose names are submitted by official WSOP sponsors, promotional partners, or licensees can be registered by a third party.

Have Your ID and Total Rewards Card With You

You'll need to positively identify yourself to register. Acceptable forms of ID are a passport, driver's license, or state or military ID card. You must also have a Total Rewards card, which is a Harrah's loyalty program card. You can get one at any Harrah's property or at the Total Rewards desk in the players' area at the WSOP.

Make Your Payment

Acceptable forms of payment include cash, Rio casino chips, cashier's check drawn from accredited banks made out in your name or the Rio, and wire transfers (five-day waiting period). Also note that you may use a credit card to get a cash advance. Wire transfers are only accepted as payment if you pre-register for an event. For details on paying by wire transfer and cashier's check, see that section in the "Resources" chapter of this book.

Get Your Table and Seat Assignments

Once you've registered, you will receive a receipt and a slip of paper stating your table and seat assignment. These assignments are drawn randomly, and you could as easily be seated next to a stranger as a world champion of poker or a poker celebrity that you see on TV. It's just the luck of the draw.

What If You Need to Cancel?

Cancellations or voids must be signed, completed and received prior to the start of a particular event. Contact the tournament office at the WSOP for a cancellation form, or get one by e-mail at harrahs.com. E-mail notification is also acceptable provided it is received and approved prior to the beginning of the event. You may also cancel at the WSOP cage before the event begins.

Now that we've covered the nitty gritty details of registering, let's move right along to playing the tournament. That's why we're here, right? To put our chips to war with friends and foes, amateurs and pros, at the world's most exciting—and yes, intimidating—poker extravaganza.

PLAYING YOUR FIRST EVENT

Playing in a World Series of Poker event is an exhilarating experience, yet it can be overwhelming and intimidating your first time around. The Amazon Room at the Rio is enormous, with thousands of people milling around, including poker celebs such as Doyle Brunson, Daniel Negreanu, Annie Duke and Phil Ivey. You'll need to block out these distractions—playing focused poker might become your biggest challenge. Properly preparing your mind and body for a long day of intense play is one of the most important things you can do to ensure your success at the tournament table.

Prepare Yourself to Win

Cruise around the Rio and the WSOP area before your day of play to get the lay of the land. Familiarize yourself with the playing areas, parking lots, restaurants and restrooms. You might even join a cash game or satellite to help yourself adjust to the sights, sounds and energy of the playing area. Do whatever it takes to get comfortable with the energy and ambience of big-league tournament poker so that the next time you enter the Amazon Room, collecting chips is all you're thinking about.

Most tournaments begin at noon, so get up early enough to eat a light breakfast. Then take a few minutes to calm the jitters that usually shake players on their first day of play at the WSOP. Plan on making the final table—clear your schedule for the full number of days required to finish the event. Having other plans or contingency arrangements may distract you, causing you to bust out early.

Your ID and your tournament entry receipt are the only things you need to bring to the event, both of which the dealer will request when you get to your assigned seat. Unlike a cash game, you *cannot* change seats. The only possible exception is when two family members or husband and wife are assigned to the same table, in which case it's up to the tournament director to make a change.

You might also want to bring a backpack or bag along to store your sunglasses, MP3 player, snacks, business cards, pens, a notebook, eye drops, gum and medications. Wear comfortable clothes and bring a jacket or sweatshirt, as it can get chilly inside the Amazon Room. Don't worry about bringing drinks. They are provided free of charge while you're playing. Cocktail servers will happily bring you just about anything from water to whiskey—a tip is appropriate if your server is friendly and efficient.

DAY OF PLAY CHECKLIST

- ID/Total Rewards card
- Tournament entry receipt
- Warm layers of clothing
- Snacks
- Approved electronic devices

Get There Early

You've probably seen Phil Hellmuth show up hours late for a televised tournament, but that's not a good idea for most players. You'll want to arrive thirty to forty-five minutes prior to start time to help calm your nerves and get you in your rhythm for play. You want to settle in as soon the tournament begins and start concentrating on winning chips. By arriving early, you'll have time to check out your table location, locate your seat, and start visualizing mountains of chips in your spot. If you have any questions, locate a dealer or floorperson and fire away.

Several minutes before start time, you will hear an announcement to take your seat. This is your last opportunity for the next two hours to grab a smoke (in designated outdoor areas only), hit the bathroom, or call your home-game buddies and tell them how you're about to bluff your way to a bracelet.

But what if you accidentally sleep in? If you arrive late to the tournament, there is no penalty other than the chips you'll lose to the blinds once the tournament begins. The blinds are small for the first few levels of play, so you won't take a huge loss. But still, it's better to get acclimated at the start of the tournament than to come in late feeling rushed and out of sync with the game.

Turn Off Your Cell Phone

Turn your cell phone to silent before you sit down to play. Step away from the table to avoid getting a penalty if you absolutely have to use your cell. In fact, no device is permitted at the table that can access the Internet, send or receive SMS texts, or is equipped with any type of communication device. Therefore, smartphones and similar devices are not allowed at the table. Approved electronic devices include iPods and other MP3 players, and noise-reducing headphones—but only until the money is reached. After the tournament has reached the payday stage, no electronic devices are permitted.

Twittering (via Twitter) is only allowed away from the table—even the godfather of poker, Doyle Brunson, has to step away from the table when he tweets. And you thought only youngsters did the tweeting! Nope, Doyle keeps his fans up to date 24/7 when he's playing an event. With all that out of the way, it's time to play some poker.

Playing Day One

You will start with triple the amount of chips of the buy-in for the event. For example, if you are playing a $1,500 no-limit hold'em event, you will start with $4,500 chips. Levels are one-hour long in most events, with a 20-minute break after every two levels.

Bathroom lines get long at breaks, but there are ample facilities to accommodate everyone. Restrooms are located near the Poker Kitchen, in the main hallway across from Will Call, and further down the main hallway outside the Rotunda in front of the Pavilion room, a short walk that will get your blood pumping.

The 20-minute breaks are a good time to grab a light snack from the food court or get some sun and fresh air. And believe me, there's plenty of sun that time of year in Las Vegas!

For every event that starts at noon, a 90-minute dinner break is scheduled at the end of six levels of play. Play will end for the day after ten levels of play and resume between 2 p.m. and 3 p.m. the following day. For events that begin at 5 p.m., you don't get dinner break, but you do get a 60-minute break after four levels of play. Play ends after eight levels of play for all 5 p.m. events and resume between 2 p.m. and 3 p.m. the following day. The exact starting times for play on Day 2 and subsequent days in a tournament will be announced in advance.

Be careful not to stuff yourself at dinner. You'll probably be hungry and a bit drained, but a big meal during the dinner break can often lead to a "food coma" that can make it hard to keep your eyes open at the table. Remember that you still have at least four more hours of play after dinner, so you will need energy and concentration. I've found that fish, fruits and vegetables fill me up without slowing me down. Famous players like Daniel Negreanu and Cindy Violette bring food from home.

Ten minutes prior to the end of each day's play, the dealer draws a random card to determine how many additional hands will be played. This procedure prevents players from stalling or holding up their play just to make it to the next day. Once the last hand is played, you'll be given a large plastic bag and asked to count your chips. You'll write your name and chip count on the bag, throw your chips in it, and seal it. You'll find out your new table and seat assignment for Day Two before you leave the WSOP playing area at the end of Day One. When you return to play the next day, voila! Your chip bag will be waiting for you at your newly assigned seat.

Meeting the Pros in Your Tournament

While you are maneuvering your way through the event, you're bound to find yourself at the same table as some of the famous pros you see on TV. Relax, they're human. Really. They're accustomed to playing with fans, so don't hesitate to strike up a conversation. This is part of the WSOP experience. Poker pros Tom McEvoy and T.J. Cloutier are especially cordial to fans, as are Greg Raymer and Chris Moneymaker.

Just don't engage the pro in the middle of a hand. The best time to approach a pro for an autograph or picture is at the *end* of a break—not while they're rushing to a restroom or food area. Try to carve out a quick chat with them just before the next level begins, as most of them return to the table a few minutes early.

If You're at the Tournament as a Spectator

Spectating is a sport of its own at the WSOP. It's first come, first serve for the premium viewing spots along the rail.

Crowds can become four or five people deep in areas where famous pros or celebs are seated. Don't try to engage players in conversation while they're at the table; interfering with game play or annoying a player will almost certainly get you barred from the Amazon room. Photography is permitted, but you may not use a flash, nor may you shoot a video.

Before a tournament begins and during breaks are your best opportunities to approach players for a picture or autograph. Several minutes before the breaks, which occur after every two levels of play, you'll hear an announcement that spectators must leave the room. Pros need to use the breaks for their personal needs, so the best time to get them is on their way back to the tournament room. Some pros and celebs are more approachable than others. Much of your success in getting their attention will depend on how successful they have been thus far in the event. The higher their chip stacks the better your chances.

THE WSOP TOURNAMENTS

LET'S PUT THE CARDS IN THE AIR!

An Invitation to the WSOP from the Tournament Director

Whether you're chasing the dream of winning a bracelet, or you just want to take advantage of satellites, cash games and small tournaments, the World Series of Poker has something for you.

You receive triple starting chips for all bracelet events, along with additional levels of play for more opportunities to win. We also offer daily $340 no-limit hold'em tournaments and $200 events each evening that give you a chance to win cash prizes. And we schedule daily one-table and multi-table satellites for all of our events at a wide range of buy-ins.

Our payout percentages guarantee players 1.75 to 2.0 times return on their buy-in just for making the money, while players cashing up to the Final Table earn more than ever before.

You won't want to miss the World Series of Poker. I'm looking forward to seeing you when we shuffle up and deal!

Jack Effel

A TYPICAL WSOP TOURNAMENT SCHEDULE

The schedule of events at the WSOP typically includes fifty-plus tournaments. About one half of them are no-limit hold'em tournaments with buy-ins from $1,000 to $10,000, as well as tournaments for many other poker games. For example, the 2010 schedule featured fifty-seven events, including twenty-seven no-limit hold'em, five limit hold'em, nine Omaha, five seven-card stud, three deuce-to-seven draw, three mixed games, and three H.O.R.S.E tournaments. Each year's schedule also includes the Ladies Champion and Seniors tournaments, as well as a $500 buy-in Casino Employees event and the Ante Up for Africa $5,000 buy-in charity tournament.

A new special event that began in 2009 was the Champion of Champions tournament, an invitational for past world champions of poker. Tom McEvoy, the 1983 champion, defeated eighteen other world champions to drive to his Las Vegas home in a 1970 Chevrolet Corvette.

The 2010 WSOP featured a special tournament titled the Tournament of Champions with a $1 million prize pool. The public was invited to vote for their favorite players from the list of all past WSOP bracelet winners, with the top twenty nominees invited to play in the event. Past Tournament of Champion winners Annie Duke, Mike Matusow, and Mike Sexton were automatically awarded entry, along with reigning WSOP champion Joe Cada, reigning WSOPE champion Barry Shulman, and two wild card exceptions.

The schedule also rolled out the Poker Player's Championship $50,000 buy-in tournament to replace the $50,000 buy-in H.O.R.S.E. event. Instead of five games, the new multigame format included no-limit hold'em, limit hold'em, Omaha high-low, pot-limit Omaha, seven-card stud high and high-low, razz, plus deuce-to-seven and triple draw lowball.

2010 WORLD SERIES OF POKER
DAILY TIME SCHEDULE
*START TIMES ARE SUBJECT TO CHANGE

THURSDAY, MAY 27, 2010

1pm:	#58:	The Poker Players Championship Mega Satellite $2250
4pm:	#60:	The Poker Players Championship Mega Satellite $2250
8pm:	#62:	The Poker Players Championship Mega Satellite $2250

FRIDAY, MAY 28, 2010

12 Noon:	#1:	Casino Employees No-Limit Hold'em $500
5pm:	#2:	The Poker Players Championship $50,000

SATURDAY, MAY 29, 2010

12 Noon:	#3A:	No-Limit Hold'em Day 1A $1,000
2:30pm:	#1:	Casino Employees Event Final Table
3pm:	#2:	The Poker Players Championship Day 2

SUNDAY, MAY 30, 2010

12 Noon:	#3B:	No-Limit Hold'em Day 1B $1,000
3pm:	#2:	The Poker Players Championship Day 3
5pm:	#4:	Omaha Hi-Low Split-8 or Better $1,500

MONDAY, MAY 31, 2010

12 Noon:	#5:	No-Limit Hold'em $1,500
2:30pm:	#3:	No-Limit Hold'em Day 2
3pm:	#2:	The Poker Players Championship Day 4
3pm:	#4:	Omaha Hi-Low Split-8 or Better Day 2

TUESDAY, JUNE 1, 2010

12 Noon:	#6:	No-Limit Hold'em Shootout $5,000
2:30pm:	#3:	No-Limit Hold'em Day 3
2:30pm:	#5:	No-Limit Hold'em Day 2
3pm:	#2:	The Poker Players Championship Final Table
3pm:	#4:	Omaha Hi-Low Split-8 or Better Final Table
5pm:	#7:	2-7 Triple Draw Lowball $2,500

WEDNESDAY, JUNE 2, 2010

12 Noon:	#8:	No-Limit Hold'em $1,500
2:30pm:	#3:	No-Limit Hold'em Final Table
2:30pm:	#5:	No-Limit Hold'em Final Table
2:30pm:	#6:	No-Limit Hold'em Shootout Day 2
3pm:	#7:	2-7 Triple Draw Lowball Day 2

(continued)

2010 WORLD SERIES OF POKER
DAILY TIME SCHEDULE
*START TIMES ARE SUBJECT TO CHANGE   *(continued)*

THURSDAY, JUNE 3, 2010

12 Noon:	#9:	Pot-Limit Hold'em $1,500
2:30pm:	*#6:*	*No-Limit Hold'em Shootout Final Table*
2:30pm:	*#8:*	*No-Limit Hold'em Day 2*
3pm:	*#7:*	*2-7 Triple Draw Lowball Final Table*
5pm:	#10:	Seven Card Stud Championship $10,000

FRIDAY, JUNE 4, 2010

12 Noon:	#11:	No-Limit Hold'em $1,500
2:30pm:	*#8:*	*No-Limit Hold'em Final Table*
2:30pm:	*#9:*	*Pot-Limit Hold'em Day 2*
3pm:	*#10:*	*Seven Card Stud Championship Day 2*
5pm:	#12:	Limit Hold'em $1,500

SATURDAY, JUNE 5, 2010

12 Noon:	#13A:	No-Limit Hold'em Day 1A $1,000
2:30pm:	*#9:*	*Pot-Limit Hold'em Final Table*
2:30pm:	*#11:*	*No-Limit Hold'em Day 2*
3pm:	*#10:*	*Seven Card Stud Championship Final Table*
3pm:	*#12:*	*Limit Hold'em Day 2*
5pm:	#14:	2-7 Draw Lowball (No-Limit) $1,500

SUNDAY, JUNE 6, 2010

12 Noon:	#13B:	No-Limit Hold'em Day 1B $1,000
2:30pm:	*#11:*	*No-Limit Hold'em Final Table*
3pm:	*#12:*	*Limit Hold'em Final Table*
3pm:	*#14:*	*2-7 Draw Lowball (No-Limit) Day 2*
5pm:	#15:	Seven Card Stud Hi-Low Split Championship $10,000

MONDAY, JUNE 7, 2010

12 Noon:	#16:	No-Limit Hold'em / Six Handed $1,500
2:30pm:	*#13:*	*No-Limit Hold'em Day 2*
3pm:	*#14:*	*2-7 Draw Lowball (No-Limit) Final Table*
3pm:	*#15:*	*Seven Card Stud Hi-Low Split Championship Day 2*

TUESDAY, JUNE 8, 2010

12 Noon:	#17:	No-Limit Hold'em $5,000
2:30pm:	*#13:*	*No-Limit Hold'em Day 3*

2010 WORLD SERIES OF POKER
DAILY TIME SCHEDULE
*START TIMES ARE SUBJECT TO CHANGE

2:30pm:	*#16:*	*No-Limit Hold'em / Six Handed Day 2*
3pm:	*#15:*	*Seven Card Stud Hi-Low Split Championship Final Table*
WEDNESDAY, JUNE 9, 2010		
12 Noon:	#18:	Limit Hold'em $2,000
2:30pm:	*#13:*	*No-Limit Hold'em Final Table*
2:30pm:	*#16:*	*No-Limit Hold'em / Six Handed Final Table*
2:30pm:	*#17:*	*No-Limit Hold'em Day 2*
5pm:	#19:	2-7 Draw Lowball (No-Limit) Championship $10,000
THURSDAY, JUNE 10, 2010		
12 Noon:	#20:	Pot-Limit Omaha $1,500
2:30pm:	*#17:*	*No-Limit Hold'em Final Table*
2:30pm:	*#18:*	*Limit Hold'em Day 2*
3pm:	*#19:*	*2-7 Draw Lowball (No-Limit) Championship Day 2*
5pm:	#21:	Seven Card Stud $1,500
FRIDAY, JUNE 11, 2010		
12 Noon:	#22:	Ladies No-Limit Hold'em Championship $1,000
2:30pm:	*#18:*	*Limit Hold'em Final Table*
2:30pm:	*#20:*	*Pot-Limit Omaha Day 2*
3pm:	*#19:*	*2-7 Draw Lowball (No-Limit) Championship Final Table*
3pm:	*#21:*	*Seven Card Stud Day 2*
5pm:	#23:	Limit Hold'em/Six Handed $2,500
SATURDAY, JUNE 12, 2010		
12 Noon:	#24A:	No-Limit Hold'em Day 1A $1,000
2:30pm:	*#20:*	*Pot-Limit Omaha Final Table*
2:30pm:	*#22:*	*Ladies No-Limit Hold'em Championship Day 2*
3pm:	*#21:*	*Seven Card Stud Final Table*
3pm:	*#23:*	*Limit Hold'em/Six Handed Day 2*
5pm:	#25:	Omaha Hi-Low Split-8 or Better Championship $10,000
SUNDAY, JUNE 13, 2010		
12 Noon:	#24B:	No-Limit Hold'em Day 1B $1,000
2:30pm:	*#22:*	*Ladies No-Limit Hold'em Championship Final Table*
3pm:	*#23:*	*Limit Hold'em/Six Handed Final Table*
3pm:	*#25:*	*Omaha Hi-Low Split-8 or Better Championship Day 2*

(continued)

2010 WORLD SERIES OF POKER
DAILY TIME SCHEDULE
*START TIMES ARE SUBJECT TO CHANGE   *(continued)*

MONDAY, JUNE 14, 2010

12 Noon:	#26:	No-Limit Hold'em /Six Handed $2,500
2:30pm:	#:24:	*No-Limit Hold'em Day 2*
3pm:	#25:	*Omaha Hi-Low Split-8 or Better Championship Final Table*
5pm:	#27:	Seven Card Stud Hi-Low-8 or Better $1,500

TUESDAY, JUNE 15, 2010

12 Noon:	#28:	Pot-Limit Omaha $2,500
2:30pm:	#24:	*No-Limit Hold'em Day 3*
2:30pm:	#26:	*No-Limit Hold'em/Six Handed Day 2*
3pm:	#27:	*Seven Card Stud Hi-Low-8 or Better Day 2*
5pm:	#29:	Limit Hold'em Championship $10,000

WEDNESDAY, JUNE 16, 2010

12 Noon:	#30:	No-Limit Hold'em $1,500
2:30pm:	#24:	*No-Limit Hold'em Final Table*
2:30pm:	#26:	*No-Limit Hold'em/Six Handed Final Table*
2:30pm:	#28:	*Pot-Limit Omaha Day 2*
3pm:	#27:	*Seven Card Stud Hi-Low-8 or Better Final Table*
3pm:	#29:	*Limit Hold'em Championship Day 2*
5pm:	#31:	H.O.R.S.E. $1,500

THURSDAY, JUNE 17, 2010

12 Noon:	#32:	No-Limit Hold'em /Six Handed $5,000
2:30pm:	#28:	*Pot-Limit Omaha Final Table*
2:30pm:	#30:	*No-Limit Hold'em Day 2*
3pm:	#29:	*Limit Hold'em Championship Final Table*
3pm:	#31:	*H.O.R.S.E. Day 2*
5pm:	#33:	Pot-Limit Hold'em/Omaha $2,500

FRIDAY, JUNE 18, 2010

12 Noon:	#34:	Seniors No-Limit Hold'em Championship $1,000
2:30pm:	#30:	*No-Limit Hold'em Final Table*
2:30pm:	#32:	*No-Limit Hold'em/Six Handed Day 2*
3pm:	#31:	*H.O.R.S.E. Final Table*
3pm:	#33:	*Pot-Limit Hold'em/Omaha Day 2*
5pm:	#35:	Heads Up No-Limit Hold'em Championship $10,000

2010 WORLD SERIES OF POKER
DAILY TIME SCHEDULE
*START TIMES ARE SUBJECT TO CHANGE

SATURDAY, JUNE 19, 2010

12 Noon:	#36A:	No-Limit Hold'em Day 1A $1,000
2:30pm:	#32:	No-Limit Hold'em / Six Handed Final Table
2:30pm:	#34:	Seniors No-Limit Hold'em Championship Day 2
3pm:	#33:	Pot-Limit Hold'em/Omaha Final Table
3pm:	#35:	Heads Up No-Limit Hold'em Championship Day 2
5pm:	#37:	H.O.R.S.E. $3,000

SUNDAY, JUNE 20, 2010

12 Noon:	#36B:	No-Limit Hold'em Day 1B $1,000
2:30pm:	#34:	Seniors No-Limit Hold'em Championship Final Table
3pm:	#35:	Heads Up No-Limit Hold'em Championship Final Table
3pm:	#37:	H.O.R.S.E. Day 2
5pm:	#38:	Pot-Limit Hold'em Championship $10,000

MONDAY, JUNE 21, 2010

12 Noon:	#39:	No-Limit Hold'em Shootout $1,500
2:30pm:	#36:	No-Limit Hold'em Day 2
3pm:	#37:	H.O.R.S.E. Final Table
3pm:	#38:	Pot-Limit Hold'em Championship Day 2
5pm:	#40:	Seven Card Razz $2,500

TUESDAY, JUNE 22, 2010

12 Noon:	#41:	Pot-Limit Omaha Hi-Low Split-8 or Better $1,500
2:30pm:	#36:	No-Limit Hold'em Day 3
2:30pm:	#39:	No-Limit Hold'em Shootout Day 2
3pm:	#38:	Pot-Limit Hold'em Championship Final Table
3pm:	#40:	Seven Card Razz Day 2

WEDNESDAY, JUNE 23, 2010

12 Noon:	#42:	No-Limit Hold'em $1,500
2:30pm:	#36:	No-Limit Hold'em Final Table
2:30pm:	#39:	No-Limit Hold'em Shootout Final Table
2:30pm:	#41:	Pot-Limit Omaha Hi-Low Split-8 or Better Day 2
3pm:	#40:	Seven Card Stud Final Table
5pm:	#43:	H.O.R.S.E. Championship $10,000

(continued)

2010 WORLD SERIES OF POKER
DAILY TIME SCHEDULE
*START TIMES ARE SUBJECT TO CHANGE   *(continued)*

THURSDAY, JUNE 24, 2010

12 Noon:	#44:	Mixed Hold'em (Limit/No-Limit) $2,500
2:30pm:	#41:	*Pot-Limit Omaha Hi-Low Split-8 or Better Final Table*
2:30pm:	#42:	*No-Limit Hold'em Day 2*
3pm:	#43:	*H.O.R.S.E. Championship Day 2*

FRIDAY, JUNE 25, 2010

12 Noon:	#45:	No-Limit Hold'em $1,500
2:30pm:	#42:	*No-Limit Hold'em Final Table*
2:30pm:	#44:	*Mixed Hold'em (Limit/No-Limit) Day 2*
3pm:	#43:	*H.O.R.S.E. Championship Final Table*
5pm:	#46:	Pot-Limit Omaha Hi-Low Split-8 or Better $5,000

SATURDAY, JUNE 26, 2010

12 Noon:	#47A:	No-Limit Hold'em Day 1A $1,000
2:30pm:	#44:	*Mixed Hold'em (Limit/No-Limit) Final Table*
2:30pm:	#45:	*No-Limit Hold'em Day 2*
3pm:	#46:	*Pot-Limit Omaha Hi-Low Split-8 or Better Day 2*
5pm:	#48:	Mixed Event $2,500

SUNDAY, JUNE 27, 2010

12 Noon:	#47B:	No-Limit Hold'em Day 1B $1,000
2:30pm:	#45:	*No-Limit Hold'em Final Table*
3pm:	#46:	*Pot-Limit Omaha Hi-Low Split-8 or Better Final Table*
3pm:	#48:	*Mixed Event Day 2*

MONDAY, JUNE 28, 2010

12 Noon:	#49:	No-Limit Hold'em $1,500
2:30pm:	#47:	*No-Limit Hold'em Day 2*
3pm:	#48:	*Mixed Event Final Table*
5pm:	#50:	Pot-Limit Omaha $5,000

TUESDAY, JUNE 29, 2010

12 Noon:	#51:	Triple Chance No-Limit Hold'em $3,000
2:30pm:	#47:	*No-Limit Hold'em Day 3*
2:30pm:	#49:	*No-Limit Hold'em Day 2*
3pm:	#50:	*Pot-Limit Omaha Day 2*

2010 WORLD SERIES OF POKER
DAILY TIME SCHEDULE
*START TIMES ARE SUBJECT TO CHANGE

WEDNESDAY, JUNE 30, 2010

12 Noon:	#52:	No-Limit Hold'em/Six Handed $25,000
2:30pm:	#47:	No-Limit Hold'em Final Table
2:30pm:	#49:	No-Limit Hold'em Final Table
2:30pm:	#51:	Triple Chance No-Limit Hold'em Day 2
3pm:	#50:	Pot-Limit Omaha Final Table
5pm:	#53:	Limit Hold'em Shootout $1,500

THURSDAY, JULY 1, 2010

12 Noon:	#54A:	No-Limit Hold'em Day 1A $1,000
2:30pm:	#51:	Triple Chance No-Limit Hold'em Final Table
2:30pm:	#52:	No-Limit Hold'em / Six Handed Day 2
3pm:	#53:	Limit Hold'em Shootout Day 2
5pm:	#55:	Pot-Limit Omaha Championship $10,000

FRIDAY, JULY 2, 2010

12 Noon:	#54B:	No-Limit Hold'em Day 1B $1,000
2:30pm:	#52:	No-Limit Hold'em/Six Handed Final Table
2:30pm:	#53:	Limit Hold'em Shootout Final Table
3pm:	#55:	Pot-Limit Omaha Championship Day 2
5pm:	#56:	No-Limit Hold'em $2,500

SATURDAY, JULY 3, 2010

2pm:	#228:	Ante Up for Africa $5,000
2:30pm:	#54:	No-Limit Hold'em Day 2
3pm:	#55:	Pot-Limit Omaha Championship Final Table
3pm:	#56:	No-Limit Hold'em Day 2

SUNDAY, JULY 4, 2010

| 2:30pm: | #54: | No-Limit Hold'em Day 3 |
| 3pm: | #56: | No-Limit Hold'em Final Table |

MONDAY, JULY 5, 2010

| 12 Noon: | #57A: | No-Limit Hold'em Championship Day 1A $10,000 |
| 2:30pm: | #54: | No-Limit Hold'em Final Table |

TUESDAY, JULY 6, 2010

| 12 Noon: | #57B: | No-Limit Hold'em Championship Day 1B $10,000 |

(continued)

WEDNESDAY, JULY 7, 2010

12 Noon:	#57C:	No-Limit Hold'em Championship Day 1C $10,000

THURSDAY, JULY 8, 2010

12 Noon:	#57D:	No-Limit Hold'em Championship Day 1D $10,000

FRIDAY, JULY 9, 2010

12 Noon:	*#57:*	*MAIN EVENT DAY 2A (1A + 1C)*

SATURDAY, JULY 10, 2010

12 Noon:	*#57:*	*MAIN EVENT DAY 2B (1B + 1D)*

SUNDAY, JULY 11, 2010

1pm:	—	Media Event – *Main Event OFF Day*

MONDAY, JULY 12, 2010

12 Noon:	*#57:*	*MAIN EVENT DAY 3*

TUESDAY, JULY 13, 2010

12 Noon:	*#57:*	*MAIN EVENT DAY 4*

WEDNESDAY, JULY 14, 2010

12 Noon:	*#57:*	*MAIN EVENT DAY 5*

THURSDAY, JULY 15, 2010

12 Noon:	*#57:*	*MAIN EVENT DAY 6*

FRIDAY, JULY 16, 2010

12 Noon:	*#57:*	*MAIN EVENT Play Down to 27*

SATURDAY, JULY 17, 2010

12 Noon:	*#57:*	*MAIN EVENT Play Down to Final 9 (November Nine)*

THE WSOPE (EUROPE) TOURNAMENTS

The World Series of Poker Europe (WSOPE) complements the WSOP Las Vegas event. During the WSOPE's first two years, a total of 1,740 entrants competed for seven gold bracelets and were awarded £9,997,500 in prize money.

The WSOPE has been held in the fall at the Casino at the Empire in Leicester Square in London, England with four gold

Barry Shulman
2009 WSOPE Champion

bracelets up for grabs. The 2009 championship event culminated in a rugged heads-up battle between Americans Barry Shulman and Daniel Negreanu. Shulman won the title plus £801,603 just a few weeks before his son Jeff Shulman placed fifth at the final table of the WSOP Main Event.

Annette Obrestad won the largest amount ever for a female in any sporting event, £1 million (U.S. $2,013,102) when she won the inaugural WSOPE Main Event in 2007. Six different nations have captured a WSOPE bracelet: Denmark (2), Afghanistan, Germany, Italy, Norway and USA.

Here is the list of WSOPE bracelet winners through 2009.

WSOPE BRACELET WINNERS		
YEAR	WINNER	EVENT
2007:	Annette Obrestad	£10,000 Main Event No-Limit Hold'em
	Thomas Bihl	£2,500 H.O.R.S.E.
	Dario Alioto	£5,000 Pot-Limit Omaha
2008:	John Juanda	£10,000 Main Event No-Limit Hold'em
	Theo Jorgensen	£5,000 Pot-Limit Omaha
	Sherkhan Farnood	£2,500 H.O.R.S.E.
	Jesper Hougaard	£1,500 No-Limit Hold'em
2009:	Barry Shulman	£10,000 Main Event No-Limit Hold'em
	Jani Vilmunen	£5,000 Pot-Limit Omaha
	Erik Cajelais	£2,500 H.O.R.S.E.
	John-Paul Kelly	£1,000 No-Limit Hold'em

THE MECHANICS OF WSOP TOURNAMENTS

All players in a poker tournament start with an equal number of chips and the play continues until one player captures all the chips in play. As players lose their chips, they are eliminated from the tournament and the remaining competitors are consolidated into fewer tables. Eventually, only the *final table* will remain.

The final table is where you get your chance to shine against in competition for the prestige, the big money, and the gold bracelet. Those last players will do battle until one player holds all the chips—the champion. Unlike a cash game where the chips are the equivalent of cash money, *tournament chips* are only valuable in the tournament and have no cash value.

THE WSOP TOURNAMENTS

Tournaments are divided into *levels* or *rounds*. Each level is marked by an increase in the blinds and/or antes, putting more pressure on players to make moves or lose their chips to inactivity. In the WSOP, levels last for one hour in the lower buy-in events, which are designed to be completed in three days or less. The levels last as long as ninety minutes to two hours for the bigger buy-in events such as the $50,000 H.O.R.S.E tournament or the $10,000 Main Event. All WSOP events are traditionally *freeze-out tournaments*—you cannot rebuy for more chips. When you lose all your chips, you also lose your seat in the tournament.

WSOP Tournament Structure

The tournament director sets up each event differently. The length of rounds and structure for increasing the blinds and antes are available on sheets that you can pick up in the playing area near the registration desk. In general, the larger the buy-in the longer the tournament. The structure sheets and the WSOP website posts the number of days the tournament should take to finish.

The tournament director also determines how many chips each player begins with (your *starting stack*). Whether you are given $200 in chips, $1,000 in chips, or $10,000 in chips, you are on a level playing field with your competitors because in a tournament, everyone starts with the same amount of chips.

WSOP Tournament Prize Pool

WSOP tournaments are structured so that approximately 10 percent of the entrants will finish in the money. The exact dollar amount of the prizes and the number of places to be paid is posted on the television monitors located throughout the playing area after the tournament has begun, as soon as the number of players and amount of the prize pool is known. As the tournament progresses, the monitors also post the number of players remaining in the tournament and the exact amounts each can win, depending upon how high they finish. The final-table participants earn the most money, with first place getting the lion's share.

One of the worst outcomes you can suffer in a tournament is getting caught on the *bubble*—that is, being the last player eliminated before the money payouts begin. If you bust out in eighty-second place and only eighty-one players are being paid, for example, you're going home empty-handed and unhappy, while every other player remaining wins money.

What's the bottom line of a big tournament with a lot of entrants? Simple. The bigger the field, the bigger the prize pool and the more players who will cash. When the starting field of an event is huge, such as the Main Event $10,000 buy-in where well over 5,000 players usually participate, the prize pool can easily be over $50 million. The popularity of all the WSOP tournaments ensures that every event will have a prize pool over $1 million. There's plenty of money to be won in any WSOP event you enter!

HOW TO GET INTO A WSOP EVENT FOR LESS

If you're not ready or can't afford to shell out $1,000, $5,000 or $10,000 for a tournament buy-in, you can win your way into an event at a fraction of the cost through satellites or megasatellites (see next section) held at the Rio during almost all days during the WSOP. Many players do exactly that, including Scotty Nguyen who rode a satellite victory all the way to the world championship in 1998! In some circumstances, non-U.S. players can earn a seat online. The WSOP does not accept registrations from online poker sites that are U.S. based or that accept bets from U.S. citizens.

In addition, through the WSOP Circuit Events held at Harrah's properties throughout the U.S. and on popular sites like Facebook and ESPN.com, free seats are often awarded as prizes for their weekly or monthly tournaments. Another great way to get into WSOP events is through a site like SpadeClub. com, a subscription-based poker site that allows you to play in as many tournaments as you can handle for a small monthly fee. You build up points to play in WSOP qualifier tournaments that award seats to WSOP events.

TYPES OF WSOP TOURNAMENTS

Here is a short list of the many forms of tournaments offered at the WSOP. Note that satellites and megasatellites, which run around the clock, are played in separate rooms from the main tournaments.

Satellites and Megasatellites

A *satellite* is a single table tournament in which the winner gains entry into a larger-buy-in tournament for a fraction of the cost.

A *megasatellite*, or *mega*, is a lower buy-in tournament featuring multiple tables and no rebuys, in which the top finishers win an entry into a large buy-in tournament for a fraction of the cost. The WSOP will issue to the winners a *lammer*, a chip that is equivalent to the buy-in for the big tournament you were playing for; you may use that lammer for a tournament entry of the equivalent cash value or trade it in for cash. The WSOP runs frequent megasatellites to allow you the opportunity to get into the Main Event for a fraction of the cost. Turbo megasatellites with ten-minute rounds as opposed to the thirty-minute levels of the regular megas are also offered.

At the 2010 WSOP, for example, megas with buy-ins of $330, $550, $1,060, and $2,080 were offered, plus a $1,060 turbo mega. Special megas were also spread, including a $1,570 six-handed mega, and a $2,250 Poker Player's Championship mega.

Heads-Up Tournaments

Top pros look forward to the heads-up championship tournament, a series of one-on-one matches where the winners move on and the losers move out. The field continues to be divided by two until only two players remain in action. The winner of that final match is crowed the champion. For example, a field of 256 players will become 128 players, then 64, 32, 16, 8, 4, 2 and then—the champion takes home the prize.

Shootout Tournaments

A *shootout tournament* is a multi-table tournament in which each table is played down to one winner. For example, in the hold'em shootout event, ten players start at a table. Only the player who finishes first moves on to the next round to compete against the other one-table winners. The winners of the second round advance to the final table, with the winner taking home the prize. If 1,000 players begin play, 100 players will move on to round two, and only 10 players will make it to round three, the final table.

Triple Chance Event

The triple chance event gives players one-third of their chips up front, plus two lammers equal to the other two-thirds of their total chips. These lammers may be used at any point during the first three levels of play by handing the lammer to the dealer who exchanges it for the equivalent value of chips.

A POKER PRIMER FOR FANS & NEW PLAYERS

This section is tailored for fans of the WSOP and new tournament poker players. I'll show you how to play the poker games offered at the World Series of Poker, plus give you valuable strategy tips so that you'll have the best chance of getting to the final table and being crowned a champion.

You'll learn the basic rules of the games, ranks of the hands, fundamentals of play, etiquette and customs, and various betting options and structures. You'll also find out about the high, low, and high-low

Mike Matusow
2002 WSOP Omaha High-Low Champion.
Author of *Checkraising the Devil*

variations that make split games so intriguing. Most of all, you'll learn how to enter the exciting WSOP tournaments—not just the preliminary ones, which are challenging and profitable, but the big one, the Main Event. You'll become a multi-millionaire and celebrity if you go all the way to the top.

HOW POKER IS PLAYED

First, let's start with basic information on how poker is played from the first hand you're dealt to the final showdown for all the chips on the table.

Poker is played with a standard deck of fifty-two cards. The ace is the best and highest card, followed in descending order by the king, queen, jack, 10, 9, 8, 7, 6, 5, 4, 3 and then the *deuce* or 2, the lowest ranked card in the deck. Unlike the game of bridge, the four suits have no basic value in determining the winning hand in poker.

All variations of poker have these five things in common:

1. All players receive an equal number of cards to start.
2. An initial wager is made after the cards are dealt. Players that match the wager can continue playing the hand, while players that don't match it will sit out of the hand. You have to pay to play!
3. More cards are usually dealt, giving active players an option to wager more money following each round of cards.
4. The winner of each hand is the player with the best hand at the end of the deal, or the last one standing if all opponents have refused to match his bets.
5. Each player in a poker game plays by himself and for himself alone against all other players.

The Object of the Game

Your goal in a poker hand is to win the money in the *pot*, the accumulation of bets in the center of the table. You can win in two ways. The first way is to have the highest-ranking hand at the *showdown*—the final act in poker, where all active players' hands are revealed to see who has the best one. The second way is to be the last player remaining. At any time before the showdown, if all opponents discard their cards, then the last active player wins the pot. When this occurs, there is no showdown, and the active player automatically wins the pot.

Players and Dealers

Tournament poker can be played with as few as two players in heads-up play, six players in short-handed or triple draw, or as many as ten players in standard hold'em and Omaha games.

In the WSOP tournaments, the house supplies a dealer, whose only role is to shuffle the deck, deal the cards, and direct the action so that the game runs smoothly. He points out whose turn it is to play and pulls bets into the pot after each round of cards. At the showdown, he declares the best hand, pushes the pot to the winning player, reshuffles the cards, and gets ready for the next deal.

In tournament variations such as hold'em, Omaha, and draw poker in which the dealer enjoys a positional advantage, a *button* is utilized to designate the dealer's imaginary position. The button rotates around the table one spot at a time in clockwise fashion so that each player has a chance to enjoy the advantages of acting last.

Tournament poker is always played with *chips* that are assigned specific values. Every player in a tournament receives an equal amount of tournament chips to start.

Your Betting Options

When it is your turn to play, you have five options:

1. **Bet:** Put chips at risk, that is, wager money, if no player has done so before you.

2. **Call:** Match a bet if one has been placed before your turn.

3. **Raise:** Increase the size of a current bet such that opponents, including the original bettor, must put

additional money into the pot to stay active in a hand.

4. **Fold:** Give up your cards and opt out of play if a bet is due and you do not wish to match it. This forfeits your chance of competing for the pot.

5. **Check:** Stay active in a hand without making a bet and risking chips. This is only possible if no bets have been made.

The first three options—bet, call, and raise—are all a form of putting chips at risk in the hope of winning the pot. Once chips are bet and due, you must match that bet to continue playing for the pot or you must fold. Checking is not an option. If no chips are due, you can stay active without cost by checking.

If a bet has been made, each active player—one who has not folded—is faced with the same options: call, fold, or raise. Those bets no longer belong to the bettors. They become the property of the pot, the communal collection of money that is up for grabs by all active players, and which will be collected by the winner or winners of the hand.

Betting continues until the last bet or raise is called by all active players, at which point the betting round is over. A player may not raise his own bet when it's his turn to bet; he may raise only another player's bet or raise.

What Betting is All About

You make bets for one of three reasons:

1. You think your hand has enough strength to win and you want to induce opponents to put more money into the pot.

2. You want to force opponents out of the pot so that the field is narrowed, since fewer players increases your chances of winning.

3. You want to induce all your opponents to fold so that you can win the pot uncontested.

How to Bet

You make your bet by either pushing the chips in front of you—an action which speaks for itself—or by verbally calling out the play, and then pushing the chips in front of you. Simply announce, "I call," "I bet," or "I raise" to clearly indicate your intention, and then push your chips out on the felt. Note that if you announce a check, bet, raise or a fold, it is binding and you're committed to the action.

You should place your bet at least six inches toward the middle, but not so far that your chips mingle with those already in the pot and cannot be distinguished from them. That is, your chips should be far enough away from your stack and the pot so that they are clearly recognized as being your bet.

To check, simply tap or knock on the table with your fingertips or hand, or announce, "I check" or "Check." To fold, push your cards face down toward the dealer. It is illegal to show your cards to active players who are competing for the pot.

WSOP Betting Etiquette & Rules

Wait for your turn to play before announcing or revealing your decision to any opponents. For example, if you know you're going to fold, you shouldn't toss your cards to the dealer before the action comes around to your position. And when you give up your hand, pass the cards to the dealer face down so that no other player can see them. If any cards are revealed to any one player, the "show one, show all" rules require that all players see them so that everyone is kept on equal footing.

Be careful not to **string bet**. A **string bet/raise** is defined as attempting a bet or raise in multiple movements that include a return to your stack without a prior verbal declaration of intent. If you are going to make a bet and plan on reaching for your stack more than once, declare the amount of your bet before you touch your chips. You also are not allowed to use visual deception intended to induce action out of turn before your action is complete. For example, you cannot grab your chips, move them forward as though you're making a bet—but not allow the chips to touch the felt—and then pull your chips back to your stack after you've seen what other players' reactions are to your movement.

Do not throw your chips into the actual pot, called *splashing the pot*. This protects all players from an opponent intentionally or unintentionally miscalling a bet. Betting properly also allows the amount of the wager to easily be verified while making it clear to all players that a bet or raise has been made.

It is improper and illegal to discuss your hand or another player's hand while a game is in progress, or to show your cards to active players who are competing for the pot. It is also very poor form to criticize other players' strategy decisions, no matter how poor they appear to be. If you think an opponent plays poorly, that's good news for you: Go win his chips.

Putting a single, oversized chip in the pot without announcing "Raise" will only count as a call. For example, if it's $25 to you, and you toss a $100 chip in front of you without declaring "Raise," that is considered a call of the $25 bet. It is not a raise. Betting with a single oversized chip and announcing "Raise," but with no verbal amount of the raise, will commit you to a bet equal to the size of the chip. Further, be sure to keep your highest denomination chips visible at all times.

The Blinds and Antes

In poker, one or more players are required to put a bet into the pot before the cards are dealt. There are two types of mandatory bets: blinds and antes. *Blind bets*, or *blinds*, are used in the hold'em, Omaha, and draw poker variations. They are required of the first two players to the left of the button (the dealer position). An *ante*, also known as a *sweetener*, is a uniform bet placed into the pot by all players before the cards are dealt. The size of the blinds and antes for each tournament are set in advance of play.

Table Stakes, Tapped Out Players, and Side Pots

What happens if you don't have enough chips to call a full bet or raise? For example, if the bet is $250 and you only have $100 in chips, you may only call for $100. The remaining $150 and all future amounts bet during the hand—except for bets by opponents that equal the $100—will be separated into a *side pot*.

A player who has no more table funds with which to bet is *tapped-out*. A tapped-out player can still receive cards until the showdown and play for the *main pot*, however he can no longer bet in this hand and has no equity in the side pot. The other active players can continue to bet against each other for the money in the side pot in addition to remaining in competition for the main pot with the tapped-out player. At the showdown, if the tapped-out player has the best hand, he receives only the money in the main pot. The player who has the best hand among the remaining players will win the side pot. Should one of the other players hold the overall best hand, that player wins both the main pot and the side pot.

If only one opponent remains when a player taps out, there is no more betting. The cards are dealt until the showdown, where the best hand wins.

The Play of the Game

If the game requires antes or blinds, these should be placed into the pot before the cards are dealt. After the dealer shuffles the cards and offers the cut, he deals cards one at a time in a clockwise rotation, until each player has received the requisite number of cards for the poker variation being played. Like the dealing of the cards, play always proceeds in a clockwise direction. The first round of betting begins with the player sitting to the immediate left of the blinds, or in the seven-card stud games, with either the high or low card opening play. Play will continue around the table, until each player in turn has acted.

In later rounds, the first player to act will vary depending on the poker variation being played. We'll cover the particulars of play under the strategy sections for each game.

BETTING STRUCTURES

Poker has three types of betting structures: limit, pot-limit, and no-limit. These structures don't change the basic way the games are played, only the amount of money that can be bet. The big difference between the three structures is the strategy. The amount you can bet changes the hands that you should play, when you should play them, and how much you should risk in any given situation.

Let's take a brief look at each betting structure.

Limit Poker

The minimum and maximum bets in limit games are strictly regulated according to the preset limits for each level of play in WSOP tournaments.

In *limit* poker, all bets are divided into a two-tier structure, such as $25/$50, $100/$200, and $150/$300, with the larger limit bets being exactly double the lower limit. In a $50/$100 betting round, for example, when the lower limit of betting is in effect, all bets and raises must be in $50 increments. When the upper range is in effect, all bets and raises must be in $100 increments.

There is a maximum of one bet and four raises per round in limit poker, even if there are only two players in the hand.

However, once the tournament becomes heads-up, there may be unlimited raises.

In the following sections that describe individual games, we will go over exactly when the lower and higher limits apply, and how that works.

No-Limit Poker

No-limit hold'em is the exciting no-holds-barred style of poker played in the WSOP Main Event. The prevailing feature of no-limit poker is that you can bet any amount up to what you have in front of you on the table anytime it is your turn. That exciting all-in call signals a player's intention to put all his chips on the line.

The minimum bet in no-limit must be at least the size of the big blind. The first raise in a betting round must be at least double the big blind, while subsequent raises must be at least the size of the previous raise. In no-limit, there is no cap to the number of raises that may be made.

Pot-Limit Poker

The minimum bet allowed in *pot-limit* is set in advance while the maximum bet allowed is defined by the size of the pot.

When playing pot-limit, you can bet the amount that is in the pot, but only what is in the pot, at any time. If the blinds are $50/$100, the first player in the pot can call the $100 big blind and raise $250 (the size of the pot including his call). The second player can call the size of the pot, or raise the size of the pot with his bet in it. For example, if there is $350 in the pot, he can call the $350, and then raise $700 for a total bet of $1,050, making the total in the pot $1,400. If a player wishes to reraise, he can call the $1,400 and raise $2,800. This is how the pot grows fast. Minimum bets and raises work exactly like those for no-limit games.

FIVE RULES OF WINNING POKER

1.	Fold when you've been beaten! Being an overall winning player has more to do with losing less when your cards don't come in the running than it has to do with the pots you win when you have the best hand!
2.	Play with starting cards that can win. The object in poker is to have the best hand at the showdown, which means that to win you must enter into the betting with hands that have a reasonable chance of winning.
3.	Play aggressive poker. Betting and raising often causes opponents to fold, giving you a "free" pot, or makes them more cautious playing against you on further betting rounds or hands.
4.	Respect position. Your position is an important consideration in whether and how to play your starting cards and then how to proceed in future betting rounds. The deeper your position, the more playable a marginal hand.
5.	Vary your play. If you're unpredictable, opponents can't get a read on you, which gives you leverage that can be turned into profits.

TYPES OF POKER GAMES

Poker is typically played as *high poker*; that is, the player with the best and highest five-card combination at the showdown wins the money in the pot. But there are also variations where the low hand wins, and some in which players compete for both ends of the spectrum—the best high hand and the best low hand.

In each variation, of course, a player can win the pot when all of his opponents fold their hands at any point before the showdown, leaving one player alone to claim the pot—even though he may not actually have held the best hand!

High Poker

The best poker hand you can hold is the royal flush, followed by a straight flush, four of a kind, full house, flush, straight, three of a kind, two pair, one pair, and high-card hand. The order in which cards are dealt or how they are displayed is irrelevant to the final value of the hand. For example, 7-7-K-A-5 is equivalent to A-K-7-7-5.

Poker hands are ranked according to the statistical frequency of making a particular hand in five cards. The more difficult it is, the higher it ranks on the scale of poker hands. Note that all poker hands eventually consist of five cards, regardless of the variation played.

High-Card Hands: A hand containing five unmatched cards, that is, lacking any of the combinations shown below, is valued by its highest ranking card. 3-9-K-7-10, is a "king-high" hand. When the highest ranking cards are identical, the next highest untied card wins. A-K-J-10-4 beats A-K-J-3-2.

One Pair: Two cards of equal rank and three unmatched cards. Example: 5-5-8-J-K. If two players are competing with one-pair hands, then the higher ranked of the pairs—aces highest, deuces lowest—wins the pot. And if two players have the same pair, then the highest side card would be used to determine the higher-ranking hand. 5-5-A-7-6 beats 5-5-K-Q-J, since the ace is a higher kicker than the king.

Two Pair: Two pairs and an unmatched card. Example: 6-6-J-J-2. The highest pair of competing two-pair hands will win, or if the top pair is tied, then the second pair. If both pairs are equivalent, then the fifth card decides the winner. K-K-3-3-6 beats J-J-8-8-Q and K-K-2-2-A, but loses to K-K-3-3-9.

Three of a Kind: Three cards of equal rank and two unmatched cards. Also called trips or a set. Example: Q-Q-Q-7-J. If two players hold a set, the higher ranked set will win, and if both players hold an equivalent set, then the highest odd card determines the winner. 7-7-7-4-2 beats 5-5-5-A-K, but loses to 7-7-7-9-5.

Straight: Five cards of mixed suits in sequence, but it may not wrap around the ace. For example, Q-J-10-9-8 of mixed suits is a straight, but Q-K-A-2-3 is not—it's simply an ace-high hand. If two players hold straights, the higher straight card at the top end of the sequence will win. J-10-9-8-7 beats 5-4-3-2-A, but would tie another player holding J-10-9-8-7.

Flush: Five cards of the same suit. Example: K-10-9-5-3, all in diamonds. If two players hold flushes, the player with the highest untied card wins. Suits have no relevance. Thus, Q-J-7-5-4 of diamonds beats Q-J-4-3-2 of spades.

Full House: Three of a kind and a pair. Example: 5-5-5-9-9. If two players hold full houses, the player with the higher three of a kind wins. J-J-J-8-8 beats 7-7-7-A-A.

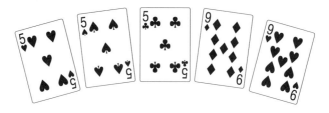

Four of a Kind: Four cards of equal rank and an odd card. Also called quads. Example: K-K-K-K-3. If two players hold quads, the higher ranking quad will win the hand. K-K-K-K-3 beats 7-7-7-7-A and K-K-K-K-2.

Straight Flush: Five cards in sequence, all in the same suit. Example: 7-6-5-4-3, all in spades. If two straight flushes are competing, the one with the highest card wins.

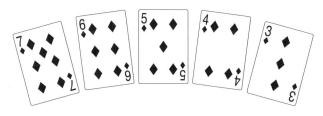

Royal Flush: The A-K-Q-J-10 of the same suit, the best hand possible. No royal flush is higher than another.

Low Poker

In *low poker*, the ranking of hands is the opposite to that of high poker, with the lowest hand being the most powerful and the highest hand being the least powerful. There are two varieties of low poker games: ace-to-five and deuce-to-seven.

In *ace-to-five*, the ace is considered the lowest and therefore most powerful card. The hand 5-4-3-2-A is the best low total possible with 6-4-3-2-A and 6-5-3-2-A being the next two best hands. Straights and flushes don't count against low hands.

In *deuce-to-seven* low poker, also known as *Kansas City lowball*, the 2 is the lowest and best card and the ace is the highest and worst. The hand 7-5-4-3-2 is the best possible hand, followed by 7-6-4-3-2 and 7-6-5-3-2. In this variation, unlike ace-to-five, straights and flushes count as high so you don't want to end up with 7-6-5-4-2 all in hearts, or 8-7-6-5-4.

High-low Poker

In high-low poker (and its variant, high-low *8-or-better*), players compete for either the highest-ranking or lowest-ranking hand, with the best of each claiming half the pot—with some restrictions, which we'll discuss in the individual games sections. With two ways to win, these games tend to be looser with more betting than other poker games. The best high hand and the best low hand split the pot, or if one player is fortunate enough to have the best high and low, he wins (*scoops*) the entire pot.

Hi-low games are sometimes played with a *qualifier*, a requirement that a player must have five unpaired cards of 8 or less to win the low end of the pot. If no player has an 8-or-better qualifier, then the best high hand will win the entire pot. For example, if the best low at the table is 9-6-5-4-2, then there is no qualified low hand and the best high hand will win the entire pot. This version of high-low poker, called *8-or-better*, is the form of high-low poker played at the WSOP tournaments.

MANAGING YOUR MONEY IN POKER

Being smart with your money is the key to becoming a winning poker player. You must exercise sound money management principles and have emotional control to handle the ups and downs. The temptation to ride a winning streak too hard or to bet wildly during a losing streak are how players beat themselves. Follow these three basic principles:

1. Only enter tournaments you can afford and that are comfortable for you.

2. Don't play when you're not at your best. If you're exhausted, annoyed, or simply frustrated by bad hands, players, or life in general, take a break. The WSOP runs tournaments every day during the championships, so there's always another tournament coming around the bend.

3. Never play with money you cannot afford to lose, either financially or emotionally. Risking funds you need for rent, food, or other essentials is foolish. The short-term possibilities of taking a loss are real, no matter how easy the tournament may appear.

This is sound money management advice. Follow it and you can never go wrong.

BASIC STRATEGY FOR WINNING WSOP HOLD'EM TOURNAMENTS

This section gives you basic strategies for the three types of hold'em games played at the World Series of Poker. Whether you're a fan or a new player, you'll learn the winning principles of tournament play. If you're a newcomer to tournament poker, use these strategies as guidelines only. Playing strictly according to the advice listed here will make your play too predictable and your opponents will take advantage of you. But don't stray too far either!

Lyle Berman
Member of Poker Hall of Fame
1989 WSOP Omaha High
Champion, Author of *I'm All In*

Keep your opponents guessing by mixing up your play, adding tricky moves in the right situations, and playing the player—cards are often secondary considerations!

In tournaments, many of your strategic decisions come from your relative chip position compared to your opponents, as well as the cost of the blinds and antes. So when you are low on chips, you'll need to play your decent hands for all they're worth in the right situations, a factor that may override specific strategy advice outlined here. In other words, how you play your hands is greatly affected by your chip count. Be flexible!

THE THREE TYPES OF TEXAS HOLD'EM

The World Series of Poker offers three different betting structures for hold'em tournaments—limit, no-limit and pot-limit.

Your final five-card hand in *Texas hold'em* will be made up of any combination of the seven cards available to you. These cards include the *board*, the five cards that are dealt face up in the middle of the table and which are shared by all players; and your *pocket cards* or *hole cards*, the two cards that are dealt to you face down that can be used by you alone.

For example, your final hand could be composed of your two pocket cards and three cards from the board, one of your pocket cards and four from the board, or simply all five board cards.

At the beginning of a hand, each player is dealt two face-down cards. Then each player gets a chance to exercise his betting options. Next, three cards are dealt simultaneously on the table for all players to share. This is called the *flop*, which is followed by another round of betting. A fourth board card, called the *turn*, is then dealt, followed by another round of betting. One final community card is dealt in the center of the table, making five total. This is the *river*. If two or more players remain in the hand, there Is a fourth and final betting round after it is dealt.

When all bets have concluded, there is the *showdown*, in which the highest ranking hand in play wins the pot.

How to Read Your Hold'em Hand

All seven cards are available to you in forming your final five-card hand—any combination of your two hole cards and the five cards from the board. You can even use all of the five board cards. Let's look at an example.

YOU HOLD

YOUR OPPONENT

THE BOARD

FLOP   **TURN**   **RIVER**

Your best hand is three jacks, which is made by using your two pocket cards and one jack from the board. Three jacks beats your opponent's pair of aces, formed with one card from his hand and one from the board. In both instances, the other cards are irrelevant. For example, there is no need to say three jacks with an ace and a king versus two aces with a king, queen, and jack—simply, three jacks versus two aces.

If the river card had been a K♦ instead of a K♣, your opponent would have a diamond flush (formed with his two pocket diamonds and the three diamonds on the board), which would beat your set of jacks.

The Play of the Game

All play and strategy in hold'em depends upon the position of the button. The player who has the button in front of him, who is also known as the button, will have the advantage of acting last in every round of betting except for the preflop round. After each hand is completed, the disk will rotate clockwise to the next player.

The player immediately to the left of the button is called the *small blind* and the one to his left is called the *big blind*. These two players are required to post bets, called *blinds*, before the cards are dealt.

The big blind is the equal to the lower bet in a limit structure, so if you're in a $50/$100 betting round, the big blind would be $50. The small blind will either be half the big blind in games where the big blind evenly divides to a whole dollar, or about one-half of the big blind when it doesn't. For example, the small blind might be $300 in a $500/$1,000 betting round.

In tournaments, the blinds will steadily increase as the event progresses, forcing you to play boldly to keep from losing your chips to inactivity.

The Order of Betting

On the preflop, the first betting round, the first player to the left of the big blind goes first. He can call the big blind to stay in competition for the pot, raise, or fold. Every player following him has the same choices: call, raise, or fold. The last player to act on the preflop is the big blind. If no raises have preceded his turn, the big blind can either end the betting in the round by calling, or he can put in a raise. However, if there are any raises in the round, the big blind and other remaining players must call or raise these bets to stay active, or they must fold.

On the other betting rounds—the flop, turn and river— the first active player to the button's left will go first and the player on the button will go last. If the button has folded, the active player sitting closest to his right will act last. When all bets and raises have been met on the flop and then the turn, or if all players check, then the next card will be dealt. On the river, after all betting action is completed, players will reveal their cards to see who has the best hand.

Betting in a round stops when the last bet or raise has been called and no bets or raises are due any player. Players cannot raise their own bets or raises.

PLAYING TIP

Never fold the big blind unless the pot has been raised. If there is no raise, there is no cost to play and you can see the flop for free.

LIMIT HOLD'EM STRATEGY

In limit hold'em, all betting is done in a two-tier structure, such as $100/$200. The three main factors to consider when deciding how to play a hand are the strength of your starting cards, where you are sitting relative to the button, and the action that precedes your play. Secondary considerations that enter into the mix are the cost of entering the pot and the aggressiveness or tightness of the table.

Your Starting Cards

The foundation of playing winning hold'em is starting with the right cards in the right positions. In early position, play only the *premium hands*—A-A, K-K, A-K, Q-Q, J-J—and raise with them. These premium hands are the best starting cards in limit hold'em and are strong enough to raise from any position at the table. You want to get more money into the pot on a hand in which you're probably leading, as well as protect that hand by narrowing the field of opponents.

In middle position, play the early position premium hands listed above plus these *playable hands*: A-Q, A-J, A-10, K-Q,

10-10, 9-9, 8-8. With the hands in the playable hands group, raise if you're the first in the pot, call if players before you have called, and fold if someone raises in front of you. Reraise if you have a premium hand.

In late position, along with the premium and playable hands, you can enter the pot with certain *marginal hands* if the pot has not been raised. These hands include small pairs—7-7, 6-6, 5-5, 4-4, 3-3, 2-2—plus K-J, Q-J, K-J, Q-10, K-10, and J-10. You may also play an ace with any other card, and suited connectors such as 5-6, 6-7, 7-8, 8-9, 9-10 of the same suit. If a raise precedes you, fold the marginal hands, call with the playable hands, and reraise with premium hands. If no one has entered the pot, raise with all premium, playable and marginal hands.

You should fold all other hands not shown in these three categories unless you're in the big blind and can see the flop for free.

The Flop and Beyond

If you don't improve on the flop, fold if it costs you to play further in the hand. For example, if an overcard flops when you have jacks, queens, or even kings, or if you miss entirely with A-K, you have to think about giving up on these hands if an opponent bets into you or check-raises. K-K is vulnerable if the flop is something similar to A-J-2.

Be careful playing flush and straight draws unless you're drawing to the *nuts*—the best hand possible given the cards on board. For example, you don't want to play a straight draw if a flush draw is also possible on the board.

NO-LIMIT HOLD'EM STRATEGY

In no-limit hold'em, your entire stack of chips is at risk on every single hand—as are those of your opponents. One big mistake and all your chips are gone. In limit hold'em, one bet is only one bet. In no-limit, that one bet could be the defining moment of your game because it could be for all your chips. And that changes the way you play hands.

Preflop Starting Hands: Early Position

The best starting cards in no-limit hold'em are the *premium hands*—A-A, K-K, Q-Q, J-J, A-K, and A-Q. In an unraised pot, usually bring these hands in for a *standard raise*—three times the size of the big blind—in early position. If the big blind is $50, make your raise $150; and if it is $100,

Barbara Enright
Only Woman to Appear at Main Event Final Table, Member of Poker Hall of Fame

make your raise $300. Your goal is to narrow the field to one or two callers and either win the pot right there when all players fold, or reduce the number of players who will see the flop.

If you have aces or kings, hopefully you'll get a caller or two, or even better, a raiser. Then you can reraise the size of the pot or go in for all your chips. With queens and A-K, you can stand a raise to see the flop, but if the raise is for all your chips, you may need to fold these hands. If you don't want your day finished with queens, you certainly don't want to go out on jacks or A-Q! If an opponent goes all-in when you hold J-J or A-Q, or even puts in a big raise, seriously consider folding these hands.

All this advice goes out the window if you're short-stacked, in which case, you're happy to make a stand with these strong hands.

If a player comes in raising before you, the aces and kings are automatic reraises and the non-premium hands are automatic folds. Lean towards calling with A-K and queens. If the raiser is tight, fold with A-Q and jacks; if the raiser is loose, raising or calling are both viable options. Remember that no play is set in stone in no-limit hold'em. You need to judge hands on a situation-by-situation basis.

Pass on all other hands from early position.

From the small or big blind position, play your hand similarly to above, however, if there are no raises, always see the flop for free from the big blind, and usually see if for one extra half bet from the small blind. You never know what you'll flop.

Preflop Starting Hands: Middle Position

If there is a raise before your turn, consider folding all non-premium hands. If the raiser is tight, fold jacks and A-Q as well. If you have A-A or K-K, reraise and have no fear of getting all your chips in the middle. You can also reraise with Q-Q and A-K, or you could just call.

If no one has raised in front of you, you still play the premium hands for a raise. And you also can add the second tier hands—10-10, 9-9 and 8-8, along with A-J, A-10, and K-Q. If you get reraised by a player behind you, consider folding second tier hands. These hands have value, but they're chip burners against heavy betting.

Preflop Starting Hands: Late Position

In you're in late position and the pot has been raised from early position, reraise with A-A, K-K, Q-Q, and A-K. If you get reraised, you may consider just calling with Q-Q and A-K; however, if the raiser is tight and goes all-in, you probably want to release these hands. And you certainly do not want to be in a reraised pot with J-J, A-Q or anything less. With aces and kings, you're always ready to play for all the marbles preflop.

If the pot is raised in middle position, reraise with the top four hands, A-A, K-K, Q-Q, and A-K. How you play jacks and A-Q is a judgment call, but it may be safer to just call and see the flop.

If no one has raised the pot, you can expand your starting hands to any pair, an ace with any other card, and any two cards 10 or higher; for example, Q-10 or K-J. Generally, it's best to come in with a raise. Most of the time, you'll win the blinds, which is good. If you get callers, you have added some value to seeing the flop.

If you are dealt aces or kings in late position and you think you'll get a caller, raise. If not, it might be better to limp in. You don't get kings or aces often, and when you do, you want to make money on them. You can also play suited connectors, such as 6-7, 7-8, 8-9, and 10-J, if you can see the flop cheaply.

HOLD'EM PREFLOP MATCHUPS (NO CARDS SHARE SUITS UNLESS SPECIFIED)			
HAND MATCHUP	HAND A WIN %	HAND B WIN %	TIE %
PAIR VS. PAIR			
A-A vs. K-K	80.79%	18.81%	.40%
A-A vs. 6-6	79.44%	20.26%	.30%
ACES VS. ACE-KING			
A-A vs. A-K	91.98%	6.80%	1.22%
A-A vs. A-K suited	87.26%	11.47%	1.27%
ACES VS. CONNECTORS			
A-A vs. J-10	81.98%	17.68%	.34%
A-A vs. J-10 suited	78.34%	21.28%	.38%
A-A vs. 6-5	81.07%	18.65%	.28%
A-A vs. 6-5 suited	76.56%	23.07%	.38%
PAIR VS. TWO OVERCARDS			
10-10 vs. A-K	56.66%	43.04%	.30%
10-10 vs. A-K suited	53.84%	45.81%	.34%
6-6 vs. A-K	55.34%	44.32%	.34%
6-6 vs. A-K suited	52.23%	47.42%	.35%
2-2 vs. J-10	50.82%	47.72%	1.46%
2-2 vs. J-10 suited	53.05%	45.54%	1.41%
PAIR VS. ONE OVERCARD (DOMINATED)			
K-K vs. A-K	69.70%	29.45%	.85%

HOLD'EM PREFLOP MATCHUPS
(NO CARDS SHARE SUITS UNLESS SPECIFIED) *(continued)*

HAND MATCHUP	HAND A WIN %	HAND B WIN %	TIE %
K-K vs. A-K suited	65.16%	34.00%	.84%
6-6 vs. 7-6	62.74%	34.42%	2.84%
6-6 vs. 7-6 suited	59.22%	37.91%	2.86%
PAIR VS. ONE OVERCARD			
K-K vs. A-Q	71.62%	28.08%	.30%
K-K vs. A-Q suited	67.48%	32.17%	.35%
10-10 vs. A-2	71.33%	28.24%	.44%
10-10 vs. A-2 suited	67.25%	32.36%	.40%
6-6 vs. A-2	69.68%	29.87%	.44%
6-6 vs. A-2 suited	65.88%	33.66%	.46%
DOMINATED HANDS			
A-K vs. A-Q	71.80%	23.71%	4.49%
A-K vs. A-Q suited	67.15%	28.30%	4.55%
A-K vs. A-6	71.27%	24.41%	4.32%
A-K vs. A-6 suited	67.32%	28.69%	3.99%
A-K vs. K-Q	73.69%	25.29%	1.02%
A-K vs. K-Q suited	69.31%	29.57%	1.11%
A-K vs. K-7	74.55%	24.39%	1.06%
A-K vs. K-7 suited	70.37%	28.45%	1.18%
TWO OVERCARDS VS. NONPAIR HAND			
A-K vs. Q-J	64.01%	35.57%	.42%
A-K vs. Q-J suited	59.98%	39.56%	.46%
A-K vs. 7-6	61.86%	37.77%	.36%
A-K vs. 7-6 suited	57.32%	42.27%	.41%
ONE OVERCARD VS. NONPAIR HAND			
A-10 vs. K-Q	59.11%	40.50%	.40%
A-10 vs. K-Q suited	55.77%	43.78%	.45%
A-2 vs. 7-6	53.45%	46.12%	.43%
A-2 vs. 7-6 suited	49.95%	49.55%	.50%

The Flop

If you came in raising preflop, you want to continue playing aggressively. If you're first to act, bet regardless of what flops. Your opponent will probably fold and you will win the pot by default. If he calls and you don't improve, you might consider checking on the turn. If he raises, it's a tough call, but you'll have to consider giving up the hand unless you believe you have better cards. If you're second, and he checks, bet out at him.

What if he bets into you? If you miss the flop, give him the pot. Since you've shown strength preflop, his bet on the flop means you're probably second-best.

When you have what you think is the best hand, your goal is to take the pot immediately, particularly when there are straight and flush draws possible; for example, if two cards of the same suit are on the board. You don't want opponents playing for another card cheaply, making it, and then destroying you with a hand that shouldn't even have seen another card. Make your opponents pay to try to beat you.

However, if you have an absolute monster like a full house or quads, you want to keep players in and extract more bets out of them. Often, that means checking and hoping that a free card will improve their hand enough to continue past the flop.

The Turn

If you've played aggressively on the preflop and flop and your opponent hasn't budged, you have to figure him for possible strength. It's time for you to look at what you think he believes you have. If you're representing strength and playing tight, you have to give him credit for a strong hand and slow down your betting. If he checks, you check, and if you're first, check to him and see how he reacts.

The River

When you have a big hand that you're confident is the best, you want to get more chips into the pot. If you're last and there have been no bets, put the amount of chips in the pot that you think your opponent will call. If you're first, you have two options: check or bet. If your opponent is very aggressive or has been leading at the pot, you can consider checking and letting him bet, then going over the top of him with a raise to try to get more chips in the pot. You want to be careful not to move an opponent off a pot with your initial bet if you want a call. Let your knowledge of how your opponent plays guide you.

When you have a strong hand, but have doubts whether it's the best one, it's often better to check at the river, rather than bet and risk a big raise that you cannot call. If your opponent checks, you'll see the showdown with no further cost. If he bets, decide what you want to do. Be careful about betting in an attempt to get an opponent to fold. He might raise you or set you all in, and you'll be forced to muck your cards and give up your chips.

If you're going to bluff at the river, however, make sure it's for enough chips so that your opponent will be faced with a tough decision on whether to call.

10 QUICK TIPS FOR NO-LIMIT HOLD'EM

by Tom McEvoy,
2009 Champion of Champions
1983 World Champion of Poker

1. NO-LIMIT HOLD'EM IS A GAME OF BIG CARDS

Big pairs and high cards are the boss hands. Playing small pairs and medium connectors is simply too expensive, unless you can play cheaply.

2. PLAY FEWER HANDS THAN YOU'D LIKE TO

To win at no-limit hold'em, you don't need to play a lot of hands, but you do need to win the majority of the hands you play. Since you can lose all your chips on one hand, trouble hands such as A-Q and K-J are often dangerous to play. Select only your best hands to get the best results.

3. BET AND RAISE THE RIGHT AMOUNT

The key to winning pots is in the betting. New players often bet too much or raise too little. Bet enough to either limit the field or build the pot. And when you have the best hand, raise an amount that you believe your opponent will call.

4. PLAY VERY FEW HANDS FROM EARLY POSITION

The earlier your position in relation to the big blind, the worse it is for you. The later your position, the better off you are. Only play your best hands up front if you want to stay in front of the pack.

5. LEARN AS MUCH AS POSSIBLE ABOUT YOUR OPPONENTS AS SOON AS POSSIBLE

Poker is a people game played with cards, not a card game played with people. You must learn how to play the same cards in a different way against different types of opponents.

6. BLUFF IN THE RIGHT SITUATIONS ONLY

Although the bluff is a major tool in no-limit hold'em, you must not bluff too often. Timing is everything. What might be a correct bluffing situation in the final stages of a tournament could get you broke in the earlier stages.

7. DON'T GET MARRIED TO A HAND

You must be able to fold a great starting hand once in a while to preserve your precious stack of chips. It doesn't matter if your opponent started with a much weaker hand than yours—if you're beaten, you must fold.

8. RAISE MORE OFTEN THAN YOU CALL

No-limit hold'em is a bettor's game not a caller's game. Anytime you make a big bet, you put your opponent to the test. Anytime your opponent makes a big bet at you, he puts you to the test. It is far better to be the tester than the tested.

9. SOMETIMES GIVE YOUR OPPONENTS MORE RESPECT THAN THEY DESERVE

Assume that your opponents know what they're doing. If this proves false, you can capitalize on their lack of skill later in the game.

10. ALWAYS PLAY SOLID POKER

Your goal in every stage of a tournament is to preserve and build your stack of chips. Always try to make the most money with your strong hands, and lose the least possible with your marginal hands. Play a solid yet aggressive strategy—and always play your A-game.

POT-LIMIT HOLD'EM STRATEGY

Like no-limit hold'em, pot-limit is a big-bet game. Every time a bet is placed into the pot, the potential for the next bettor to raise the stakes grows exponentially.

The main difference between no-limit and pot-limit hold'em is that, because of the size of the bets that you are forced to make in pot-limit, you cannot run people out of the pot with a big bet like you can in no-limit. No-limit hold'em is an aggressive game, whereas pot-limit is a semi-aggressive game. Your main goal in pot-limit hold'em is maximizing the amount of money that you can win on a hand. The purpose of raising is to build the pot, not limit the field.

Pot-limit gives you a chance to play little pairs and small connectors for a minimum amount of money, depending upon your position, the size of your pair or connectors, and the action in front of you. You might play hands like deuces, threes, fours or fives from fifth position or later. Or you might play 4-5 suited on the button when the pot has been raised, three or four people have called the pot, and it costs you only the amount of the minimum raise to see the flop. If you don't flop to your small connectors or pairs, they are easy hands to fold.

The big-card starting hands include A-A, K-K, Q-Q, J-J, 10-10 and A-K. If you can get in for a cheap price, you also might play an ace-small suited. From an early position, you should have A-Q suited or higher. From fifth position and later, you might play A-J or A-10 suited. And from late position into the blinds, you can play K-10 suited and better.

In pot-limit tournaments, there is never an ante. For that reason, picking up pots in tournaments does not have the value that it does in no-limit hold'em because, without the antes, there isn't as much to steal preflop in pot-limit.

VIII BASIC STRATEGY FOR WINNING WSOP OMAHA TOURNAMENTS

Omaha has a well-deserved reputation as a game for action players. Pot sizes tend to get large as players liberally splash chips around the table, especially in the high-low variations where multiway pots and frequent raising make the game very exciting.

Omaha high, also called *Omaha*, is a high poker game that is played exactly like hold'em, except for two things. First, players are dealt four cards to start with, as opposed to just two in hold'em. Second—and this is the part that confuses new players—you must use exactly two of your pocket cards—no more and no less—and three cards from the board to form your final five-card hand. It is easy for new players to get confused, and even world-class players have been known to misread their hands in Omaha. For example, if you were dealt four aces in the hole, you wouldn't have quads because only two of the aces would count toward the final hand. Three cards always have to come from the board to compose your final hand.

Omaha can also be played as high-low in a variation called *Omaha high-low split 8-or-better*, or simply *Omaha high-low*. In the high-low version, the best low hand and the best high hand split the pot. However, if no hand qualifies for low—five unpaired cards that are 8 or lower—the best high hand scoops (wins) the entire pot. Players can choose two different five-card combinations to make their final hands, one for the high hand

and one for the low hand. The best high hand and best low hand can be held by the same player.

Omaha is played with a button, which moves clockwise around the table after each deal, as well as a small blind and a big blind. The deal starts with each player receiving four downcards, called pocket cards or hole cards. The first betting round proceeds exactly as in hold'em, with the player to the left of the big blind acting first. When the betting action has been completed on the preflop round, the flop of three community cards is turned face-up in the center of the table, and is followed by a round of betting. The turn and river are dealt in similar fashion, each followed by a betting round. At the showdown, the highest hand wins the pot.

In limit games, all bets in the first round must be in the lower increment: for example, $50 in a $50/$100 betting round. If you were playing pot-limit, then you could bet up to the amount in the pot, and if no-limit were being played, your maximum bet would be limited only by the amount of chips you had on the table. In limit games, betting on the turn and the river must be at the higher level of the betting structure; for example, $100 in a $50/$100 betting round. In pot-limit, you can bet up to the size of the pot, and in no-limit, you can bet all your chips if you desire.

Note that unlike the other hold'em events, Omaha tournaments do not use an ante. Every level is marked by an increase in the blinds only.

POT-LIMIT OMAHA
HIGH STRATEGY

Pot-limit Omaha is the only poker game in which you might throw away the nuts on the flop and be correct in doing so. For example, suppose you flop top set, but two suited cards and two connectors are showing on the board. Although you can still play the hand, you could easily lose with it, especially against aggressive opponents with drawing hands.

Some of the best starting hands in pot-limit Omaha are aces with two high connecting cards, such as A-A-K-Q and A-A-J-10 double-suited; A-A-K-K and other hands with aces and a big pair; rundown hands that have four connecting cards (such as J-10-9-8); two bare aces without connectors (for a minimum bet); two bare kings without connectors (for a minimum bet); and three rundown cards with a pair (such as 7-7-6-5).

Before the flop, position is not as important as starting hand selection in pot-limit Omaha. After the flop, however, position becomes more important, especially in tournaments, because good position allows you to put more pressure on the pot. An important factor to consider when deciding whether to play a hand is whether your cards are strong enough to call a raise.

Many expert players believe that almost no hand is worth raising preflop in tournament play because of the large amount of tournament chips you must commit before you see any board cards. Also, your opponents will know that you have a strong hand and will play accordingly, while you won't know for sure what they're holding.

Generally speaking, no one comes in for a raise that is less than the size of the pot. You don't see $500 in the pot and bet $100 at it. In other words, don't make a small bet to try to pick up a big pot. In pot-limit Omaha, it is okay to simply announce, "I bet the pot." Then the dealer counts it down for you.

Playing on the Flop

Once the flop is dealt, you have seen seven of the nine cards from which you will make your final hand. Therefore, your big decisions are made on the flop, even more so than in two-card hold'em games, because you have much more information in front of you. With four cards in each hand, you'll find more multiway pots in Omaha than in hold'em. In pot-limit, multiway pots are usually three-handed or four-handed.

A lot of people will call a modest preflop raise and then fold on the flop. This often happens when three or four people call the raise and create a big pot. You have to flop a big hand to be able to afford to continue; you cannot play a marginal drawing hand. In other words, more players may see the flop in pot-limit Omaha, but a lot fewer players stay to see the river card.

Having a Second Draw

Ideally, you either flop the nuts or have a draw to it, especially in multiway pots. For example, suppose you have 10♠ 10♣ 9♦ 8♠ and the flop comes 10♥ 7♠ 6♣. This is a huge flop: You have the nut straight and top set. You could fill up and win if someone else has a lower set.

The action usually thins down to two or three players on the turn. If you make the nuts on the turn, you bet that too. And if anyone bets into you, you usually will raise. If you make your draw on the turn, you bet it. Just as you don't usually give free cards on the flop, you don't give them going into fifth street either. If you make it, bet it.

On the river, most players will shut down if they have been betting a big hand and the river card makes a better hand possible. It isn't a good practice to have to fold on the river, but you might have been drawing to a monster double-draw and missed everything at the end. In that case, most experts agree that the best play is to simply fold against a bet rather than try to bluff.

OMAHA HIGH-LOW SPLIT 8-OR-BETTER STRATEGY

With both a high half and low half to go after, many players stay interested in the pot, and will chase hands right

Annie Duke
2010 National Heads-Up Champion,
2009 WSOP Omaha High-Low Champion

to the river since the last card dealt can so dramatically change the complexion of a hand. Be careful not to get sucked into the loose betting that often occurs in 8-or better unless your hand is worthy of all the action. Speculation and loose play can lose you a bunch of chips in a hurry in this game.

How to Read an Omaha High-low Hand

Here is an example showing how a high and low hand is made in conjunction with the board. If you hold A-A-J-4 with a board of A-J-7-6-2, two aces from your pocket cards are used to form the high hand, A-A-A-J-7. The ace and 4 would be combined with the 7-6-2 of the board to form a 7-6-4-2-A for low. Note that in both instances, two of your downcards and three community cards are used to make the final poker hand.

YOU

BOARD

YOUR FINAL HIGH HAND

YOUR FINAL LOW HAND

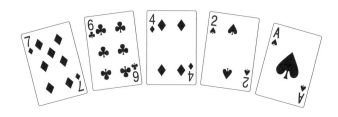

Note that you don't have a full house of aces over jacks for the high hand because you can use only two of your hole cards. If your opponent holds 3-3-3-J, he would lose on the high end since he only has a pair of jacks. Since he must use his jack as part of the hand, he does not have a 7-6-3-2-A low, so he would lose on the low end as well.

Getting Quartered

In Omaha high-low 8-or-better, players often split the pot at the showdown. In fact, there can be multiple split pots. For example, if two low hands are tied for best and there is a high-hand winner, the high hand will take half the pot, and the two low players will get *quartered*—meaning each of them will split the low half, getting just one quarter each of the total pot.

If there are three low winners, they would split the low end three ways, getting one-sixth of the pot each, with the high winner taking sole possession of the high half of the pot. Ties for the best high hand are divided the same way—all winners get an equal portion from the high half of the pot or from the whole pot if no player qualifies for low.

For there to be a winner on the low end, that hand must be no worse than five unpaired cards that are 8 or lower. For example, the hand 8-7-5-3-A qualifies for low, but the hand 8-7-5-2-2 does not qualify for low because of the paired deuces. A hand of 9-7-3-2-A would not qualify either, even though it may be the lowest hand, because the 9-high hand doesn't meet the 8-or-better qualifier. In this case, the high-end winner or winners would get all the spoils.

Here are four key concepts to keep in mind:

1. SCOOPING THE POT

In high-low games of any type, one guiding principle is the foundation of all winning strategies: play hands that have a chance to scoop the pot, that is, win both the high and low half of the pot. This is especially true in Omaha, particularly pot-limit versions.

2. PLAYING ACES

The best card in Omaha 8-or-better is the ace. Generally speaking, if you don't have one, you're better off not getting involved in the pot. While there are hands that have good potential without the ace, if you're a beginner, you can get away without playing any of them and still play a pretty solid game.

3. PLAYING GOOD STARTING HANDS

The best starters in Omaha 8-or-better have both high and low possibilities, so along with an ace plus a 2 or a 3, and a third low card, you'd like another ace (A-A-3-5), or two suited cards, preferably led by the ace, so that you have a shot at a nut flush. A king is a good card to accompany the ace, for example A-2-5-K, because it's the top kicker to an ace hand with nut-high and nut-low straight possibilities.

Four low cards such as A-2-3-4, A-2-3-5, and A-2-4-5, with two suited cards give you a decent chance of making a wheel, A-2-3-4-5 (the perfect low hand), or making a flush for a strong high hand.

When competing for the high end of the pot, hands with A-K and A-A have more strength against fewer players and less value against more players, because straights, flushes, and full houses are more common when more people stay to the end. You can start with some high-only hands, but if you do, all four of the cards must be coordinated, that is close in rank to one another. Thus, a hand like K-K-Q-J would be good, but K-K-Q-7 would not. The 7 is a "dangler" (a description originally used by T.J. Cloutier) that doesn't coordinate with the other cards.

4. PLAYING FOR THE NUTS

With so many players seeing the flop and playing through to the river, it is important that you start out with hands that have the potential to be the nuts, the best hand possible given the cards on board. For example, if you can make a flush, it should be the best flush possible (one led by an ace). When you're going for low, your hand should have the potential to be the best possible low.

The Flop and Beyond

The more players who see the flop, the better your hand must be. In particular, you either need to have the nuts or a draw to the nuts, because with the loose action common in many games, that's what it's going to take to win. When making your decision on how to play a high hand, you must consider that the pot is only worth half of what you might normally expect if a low possibility is on board. The dilution of the pot is something that regular high or low players often overlook, but it affects betting and playing strategy. That is why hands with the strength to go both ways are so valuable in high-low games.

KEY TIP FOR THE HIGH END OF THE POT

If fewer than three low cards are on board, no low hand is possible, so the high hand will scoop the whole pot.

When making your decision on how to play a high hand, you must consider that the pot is only worth half of what you might normally expect if a low hand is possible. The dilution of the pot is something that regular high or low players often overlook, but it affects betting and playing strategy. That is why hands with the strength to go both ways are so valuable in high-low games.

If you don't connect with the flop, especially with high-only cards, fold your hand. If you do connect, make sure your hand is going toward the nuts and not second best. With more betting rounds to come, you don't want to be putting in a lot of chips unless you have a hand that can go all the way.

BASIC STRATEGY FOR WINNING WSOP DRAW POKER TOURNAMENTS

The WSOP offers two forms of draw poker tournaments: deuce-to-seven lowball and triple draw. These interesting draw poker variations present a different twist to poker. Both variations are played as deuce-to-seven lowball, where the lowest hand is the strongest, as opposed to the standard high poker games in which the highest hand is the best. In deuce-to-seven, holding an ace is poison. Thus, 7-6-5-4-3 (a straight), and A-6-5-4-3 are terrible hands, beaten by the "lowly" hand of K-Q-J-9-8. And a 7-5-4-3-2 hand in clubs, a flush, loses to 4-4-4-K-Q!

In deuce-to-seven low poker, the lowest and best card is a deuce and the highest, and therefore worst, is an ace. Flushes and straights count against the player, so the best hand is 7-5-4-3-2 of mixed suits, with 7-6-4-3-2, 7-6-5-3-2, and 7-6-5-4-2 being the next three best hands.

HOW TO PLAY

In both draw poker games, each player is dealt five face-down cards to start and the action begins with the first player to the left of the big blind. He must either call the big blind bet or raise, or he must fold. Each player thereafter is faced with the same choices—call, raise, or fold.

After the first round of action is completed, there is a *draw*, where active players, those who have not folded, can exchange unwanted cards for new ones. You may exchange up to five cards, or you can exchange no cards at all and stand pat. The draw occurs in the same order as the betting, beginning with the first active player to the left of the button. The cards should be tossed face down toward the dealer, who will issue an equivalent number of new cards from the unused portion of the deck. You should draw in turn, waiting for the previous player to receive his new cards before making your own discards. The button draws last, if he is still in the pot.

A second round of betting follows. The first player to act may check or bet, and the betting will proceed around the table until all the bets have been completed. Once an opening bet is made, checking is no longer permitted. Subsequent players must call (or raise), or they must fold.

This is the point where the two draw poker variations differ. In single draw deuce-to-seven, the drawing and betting is over and there is the showdown, where the *lowest* hand wins the pot and gets to rake in the chips. In triple draw, a fun variant of deuce-to-seven low poker, the action doesn't stop after one draw. There are two more drawing and betting rounds, played exactly like the initial round, with the showdown occurring after the last round. Triple draw features a total of four betting rounds—one when the cards are dealt, and one after each of the three drawing rounds—as opposed to the straight draw poker variations, where there are just two betting rounds, one before the draw and one after. Because of the number of cards needed for three rounds of drawing, triple draw is played by a maximum of six players.

Tournament deuce-to-seven lowball poker is played with an ante and two blinds—a small blind immediately to the left of the button, and a big blind to that player's left.

The WSOP triple draw tournaments, like hold'em and Omaha, use a button to mark the dealer position, and are played with a small blind and big blind to stimulate action—but no ante as in the single draw variation.

DEUCE-TO-SEVEN LOWBALL STRATEGY

Knowledgeable players have a tremendous advantage over beginners at this variation of lowball, since the strategic thinking is vastly different from high poker. In lowball, players are shooting for different types of hands, and it takes the high poker player some time to become accustomed to the peculiarities of playing low hands.

Jennifer Harman
2002 WSOP Limit Hold'em
Champion,
1999 Deuce-to-Seven
Champion

A jack-high hand is a favorite over any hand that is taking a one-card draw and a huge favorite over a hand drawing two cards. If you draw last against an opponent drawing one card, you can consider standing pat; in the long run, you have the winning hand. And if an opponent draws two cards, don't even think about taking a draw with a jack high. With all the pair cards and high cards he can draw, you have an enormous edge. Also, if you have a jack-high hand, don't break it up for a one-card draw unless you can significantly improve. For example, breaking up J-10-4-3-2, best case scenario, only gets you to a 10-high hand. But breaking up J-7-5-3-2 can improve you to a 7-high hand, a considerably stronger draw than the J-10.

What if you have to draw first? Now you have a tougher decision on how best to play your hand. This is a good illustration of the power of position in lowball draw poker. That is why you want to play tighter in early position, in other words, entering the pot with stronger hands than if you're in late position. The later your position, the weaker your hands can be to enter the pot. Up front, in early position, throw away two-card drawing hands, though consider them payable if you can steal with them in late position, particularly if the blinds and antes are high. But make sure that two-card draw has a deuce—or throw it away.

Keep in mind that starting cards like 6-5-4-3 are terrible because the best card you can draw is an 8, giving you a weak 8-led hand, while the draw of a 2 or a 7 gives you a straight—and that's pretty bad in deuce-to-seven.

The best drawing hand you can have is 7-4-3-2 offsuit, and second best is 7-5-3-2, though 5-4-3-2 is pretty good too. Note that aces are always high in deuce-to-seven, so the draw of an ace to 2-3-4-5 is not as bad as it first appears. Your A-2-3-4-5 hand is *not* a straight, but an ace-high hand, which will beat any player who pairs. There are so many bad draws you can get by drawing even just one card—for example, it is 4.9 to 1 against having a 7-low hand starting with 7-6-3-2—that deuce-to-seven lowball is a game where position, aggression and bluffing are king.

TRIPLE DRAW STRATEGY

In triple draw, the first thing to keep in mind is that, with the four rounds of play, there is a tremendous amount of action. Given the number of bets you'll have to face to see the showdown, you need to be careful about the hands you choose to play and be prepared for big swings in your bankroll.

You also need to adjust your way of thinking if you're accustomed to playing ace-to-five lowball. For one, the ace is not the best card—it's the worst one. For another, you may end up with what you think is a great hand, only to realize that you're stuck with a straight or flush at the showdown! This results in a lot of lost chips. And unfortunately, these chips are going from you to your opponent, not the other way around.

So the first step toward acclimating yourself to this game is to realize that the deuce is boss. When you start out with a deuce, you have the potential for a great hand, and when you don't, you're working with a big handicap and should consider folding, especially against heavy betting.

Playing garbage in triple draw will soon divest you of a large portion of your chips, so your starting hand requirements must be strict. There are five types of starting hands: pat hands, one-card draws, two-card draws, three-card draws, and "the rest."

Pat Hands

If you're dealt a five-card hand led by an 8 or, even better, a 7, you should put in every bet you can in each round. Unlike other games, it is hard to disguise a big pat hand in triple draw because once it comes to the draw and no cards are taken, it is no mystery that you're representing a big hand. A pat 8 can be vulnerable, but early on in the rounds, it is a probable favorite.

One-Card Draws

One-card draws to the 7 and 8 are strong and should be played aggressively; for example, K-7-5-3-2, K-6-4-3-2, Q-7-6-4-2, and A-8-5-4-3. You want to narrow the field by raising, thereby giving opponents fewer chances to get lucky and draw out on your cards. Your one-card draw is likely a better hand than any opponent currently holds, and you want those cards to stay in the lead. If you're drawing to the wheel (7-5-4-3-

2), the best possible hand, you want opponents to stay in the pot, so you should play more conservatively. An exception to playing one-card 8-draws is when a straight draw is possible, in which case your hand has problems. For example, A-8-7-6-5 and Q-8-6-5-4 reduces the number of good cards you can catch to two, as opposed to Q-8-6-5-2, which gives you three good cards to catch.

If your five-card hand is led by a 9, and backed by strong cards, such as a 9-7-4-3-2, you have three draws to improve to a great hand. However, if your 9 is backed by big cards, such as 9-8-7-6-3, you have a hand that may be better thrown away.

Two-Card Draws

Most of the time you'll be drawing two cards to your hand, but you'll want to make this two-card draw to a good hand. Any three cards 7 or less which contains a 2 are strong, particularly 2-3-4 and 2-3-7, which are your best starting three-card hands. Two-card draws 7 or less with a 3 are less valuable, and should be dropped against heavy opposition, though they can be played against a late position player trying to steal your blind. Without the deuce, these hands drop in value, so on the draw, you're hoping to get a deuce to improve.

Three-Card Draws

For three-card draws, the 2 must be one of those cards, along with a 3, 4, 5, or 7 (but not a 6, which is problematic). Otherwise, your hand is simply unplayable. Drawing three cards is a longshot, so you should make this play only if no one has entered the pot and you are in a steal position, or if you are defending the blind from a late position player you suspect of stealing. If you don't get at least one low card on the draw to improve your hand, you'll probably need to fold to any betting.

Four- or Five-Card Draws

If you need a four- or five-card draw to improve your position, muck your cards and wait for the next hand.

Other Strategy Considerations

The button acts last in every betting and playing round in triple draw, so like hold'em, position is extremely important. Pay attention to the number of cards opponents take before you have to draw, and watch how they bet before you commit any chips to the pot. If you were able to get position every hand you played, you would have an enormous advantage over opponents, especially since you'd not only be able to see the number of cards they draw before you have to make this decision yourself—as you would in other draw poker variations—but you'd get this advantage on four betting rounds!

Whenever an opponent draws more cards than you, bet and force him to play for more chips. You have a big advantage and want more chips in the pot. Your opponents have that many more cards that could come bad, either high-carding or pairing their hands. If you draw more cards than your opponents, then the situation is reversed. Unless you improve, you should check in order to minimize the betting.

If you draw the same number of cards and improve, play aggressively. If you don't improve and go first, check. If opponents go first and bet, consider folding.

On the last draw, you have to keep in mind that your final draw could easily give you a pair, high card, straight, or flush, destroying a hand that was a strong four-card draw. For example, a 7-5-3-2, could turn into a woeful A-7-5-3-2 or even worse, 7-7-5-3-2. But you could also draw one of two great cards, a 6 or a 4, with an 8 being very strong and a 9, playable. Compare that to the hand 5-4-3-2 which gives you only one great card, a 7, one very strong card, an 8, and one playable card, a 9. The 6 would be a disaster, giving you a straight. 6-5-

4-3 is even worse. This hand has nowhere to go. A draw of a 7 or a 2 destroys the hand by forming a straight, leaving you only with an 8 to make a relatively high 8.

On the last draw, if your opponent is drawing a card, a 9-high hand is a big favorite. In fact, if you have a five-card jack or better, you are a slight favorite over any opponent who has to draw one card. If your opponent draws first, you can consider staying pat with a jack-high hand because you're in the lead. However, if you go first with that same jack-high hand, you won't know what your opponent will do, so you should draw if your jack or 10 is backed by a four-card 8 or 7, and hope that your low improves. If you have a 9, you'll have to see how the action goes then decide whether a draw is needed. If your opponent stayed pat the draw before and you have a chance to improve, you'll probably need to take a card.

Always keep in mind that any one-card draw—either yours or your opponent's—can go down in flames with a bad card on the end. Until a made low is formed, the possibility of a disastrous draw is a risk in all the low poker variations.

BASIC STRATEGY FOR WINNING WSOP SEVEN-CARD STUD TOURNAMENTS

Seven-card stud's three main variations—high, low, and hi-low—pack five exciting betting rounds into play. In each variation, players form their best five-card combination out of the seven dealt to produce their final hands.

Players will receive a total of seven cards if they play through to the end. After the first three cards are dealt (two *face-down*, or *closed*, and one *face-up*, or *open*), the first betting round commences. The following three cards—the fourth, fifth and sixth—are dealt open, one at a time, to each active player, with a betting round accompanying each card. The last card, the seventh, comes "down and dirty," that is, face down.

All players who have not folded now hold three hole cards and four open cards. A final round of betting follows the seventh card, and then the showdown occurs with the best hand (or hands, as may be the case in hi-low) claiming the pot. In each variation of seven-card stud, a player can also win the pot before the showdown by forcing out all opponents through bets and raises that opponents won't match.

In *seven-card high stud*, the highest-ranking hand at the showdown wins the pot. In *razz* (also called seven-card low stud), the lowest hand claims the gold. In *seven card stud high-low 8-or-better*), players vie for either the highest-ranking or lowest-ranking hand, with the best of each claiming half the pot—with some restrictions.

SEVEN-CARD STUD: PLAY OF THE GAME

The player holding the lowest open card will make the *bring-in*, the forced opening bet that starts the action on *third street*, the first round of betting—so named for the three cards that each player holds. If two players have identically ranked cards, the player with the lower ranked suit plays first. For this purpose only, the suits are ranked, with clubs being the lowest, followed by diamonds, hearts, and spades. For example, if the lowest ranked open cards are the 3♦ and the 3♠, the 3♦ will open the betting.

In all WSOP tournament seven-card stud variations, each players must place an ante before the cards are dealt, and additionally, the highest or lowest card on board must make a bring-in bet, depending upon the variation.

The bring-in bet will be less than the size of the smaller bet in a tournament round. For example, in a $200/$400 round, the bring-in might be $50, and in a $300/$600, it might be $100—see the tournament structure sheets, or simply follow the dealer instructions to know what the bring-in bet will be for each level of play.

The first player to the bring-in's left plays next, and he must either *complete* the bet, that is, bring it up to the lower limit of the betting structure (so if it's a $200/$400 round, then he must make it a total of $200 to call). He can also raise the completed bring-in, making it $400 total (the $200 bring-in plus the $200 raise), or fold. Play moves around the table until all bets and raises have been called. Or it will end right there if no player chooses to call the bring-in, giving the bring-in bettor the pot. There is no checking on third street.

All bets and raises in the first betting round are at the lower limit of the betting tier, $200 in this example.

When third-street betting is completed, each active player receives a face-up card. Everyone now holds a total of four cards, two open and two closed. Play in this round, called *fourth street*, and all following rounds, begins with the best open hand and moves clockwise around the table. When two or more players hold identically ranked cards, the player closest to the dealer's left plays first. If players held K-K, A-Q, and 6-6 in a high or high-low game, the pair of kings would lead off the betting.

Beginning on fourth street and continuing through the last betting round, the first bettor to act may check to open the betting since there is no bring-in bet to meet. All bets and raises on fourth street are in the lower limit unless an open pair shows on board, in which case players may elect to open with a bet from the upper limit of the betting. Thus, on fourth street in a $200/$400 betting round, bets would be $200, unless an open pair forms on board, in which case $400 could be bet.

Once fourth-street betting is concluded, another open card is dealt to each active player. This round is called *fifth street*, and all bets and raises on this round and in the following two rounds, sixth and seventh streets, are in the upper tier of the betting limit. Bets and raises would now be $50 in this round.

This next betting round is called *sixth street* and is played the same as fifth street. *Seventh street* is the final betting round. Each remaining player receives his seventh and final card face down. There is a round of betting, which is followed by the showdown if two or more player remain.

RAZZ: PLAY OF THE GAME

Unlike the WSOP draw poker tournaments, which are played as deuce-to-seven lowball, razz is played as ace-to-five lowball. In ace-to-five, the ace is the lowest and best card, and forming straights and flushes doesn't count against you.

Low seven-card stud, razz, is played identically to high stud except that the player with the highest ranking open card makes the bring-in bet on third street. If two players have identically ranked cards, the player with the higher ranked suit plays first. On fourth street and thereafter, the lowest-ranked hand—or if two players have equivalent low hands, the one closest to the dealer's left—will open betting.

Like seven-card stud high, there is an ante every betting round, and the completion bet will be at the lower tier of the preset levels for every betting round.

SEVEN-CARD STUD HIGH-LOW SPLIT 8-OR-BETTER

The betting structure in high-low split 8-or-better is identical to high stud, with the low card bringing it in, and the completion of the bet being at the lower tier of the preset level for that betting round. The betting amount rises to the upper tier of the preset level on fifth street (the third open card on board for each player, their fifth overall card)—unlike the high version, betting does not go into the upper tier if an open pair appears on board.

SEVEN-CARD STUD HIGH STRATEGY

Phil Ivey
2009 WSOP Double Bracelet
Winner

The first three cards you receive in seven-card stud lay the groundwork for the future possibilities of your hand. Therefore, to build winners, you should only stay in with cards that have the right ingredients. Starting and staying with promising cards is especially important in seven-card stud, since the five betting rounds of this game add up to a lot of bets and raises.

MINIMUM SUGGESTED STARTING CARDS

Three of a kind
Three-card straight flush
Three-card flush
Three-card straight
Pair of tens or higher
Low or middle pair with ace or king kicker
Concealed pair with face card kicker
Three high cards, two of them suited

With *three of a kind*, you are heavily favored to win and want to keep as many players in the pot as possible. Play low-key on third and fourth street, calling bets but not raising. With *three-card flushes and straights*, call third street betting, but do not raise. If your draw doesn't improve by fourth street, fold the hand. *Pairs of tens or higher* should be played aggressively to narrow the field, particularly aces, and kings and queens, if they have no card higher showing on the board. Play *low and middle pairs* only with an ace or a king as a side card. If you pair up the ace or king, it gives you a good chance to win, unless you have the kings and an opponent shows an ace. *Concealed pairs with a face card kicker* give you hidden strength while *three high cards with two of them suited* are good drawing hands.

You must pay attention to all the open cards in seven-card stud. Cards in play obviously cannot be drawn and therefore greatly impact the chances that you or your opponent will improve your hand. If you hold a marginal hand and are unsure of how to proceed, lean toward folding if cards you need are already in play, and lean toward playing if they are not.

A key factor to winning at seven-card stud, as in any poker game, is making sure you lose as little as possible in the pots you don't win. Fold hands that have not panned out or have become underdogs. Avoid the temptation to play "just one more card." Usually, it costs money and if it's not a sound call, that bet is deducted from your stack.

RAZZ STRATEGY

In razz, you use your best five cards out of the seven dealt to form the *lowest* possible hand. Strategic thinking in razz is different than in standard seven-card stud. Unlike high poker, where players sometimes start with strong hands, good lowball hands always start out as *drawing hands* that need improvement to develop into winners.

Your first four cards may be A-2-3-4, a golden start, but if the next three cards you receive are two jacks and a king, then your hand melts into nothing. On the other hand, seven-card high stud presents situations where you're dealt big hands for starters, such as the starting hand Q-Q-Q, and regardless of the next four cards, your trip queens are heavily favored to win. Subsequent draws cannot diminish the inherent strength of this high hand. In contrast, lowball hands that don't improve die on the vine and become worthless.

Here are the minimum opening or calling hands that should be played in razz.

RAZZ MINIMUM SUGGESTED STARTING CARDS
Three-card 7-high or better (lower)
Three-card 8-high with two cards valued 5 or lower
Three-card 9-high with two of the other three cards being an ace, 2, or 3
An ace plus a 5 or a lower card, and an odd card

If you don't hold one of the above combinations, you should fold. You don't want to play underdog cards and contribute to other players' pots. If you can get a free ride into fourth street, take it, but hands weaker than those shown above should not call a blind or opening bet. However, if you're the blind, and no raises occur behind your position, you're already in—take the free card.

Hands with relatively low supporting cards are called *smooth* hands. For example, the 3-2 in the starting hand of 7-3-2, a smooth seven, or the 4-3-2-A in the hand 8-4-3-2-A, a smooth 8. Hands where the supporting cards are relatively high are called *rough*, such as the 6-4 in the starting cards 7-6-4, called a rough 7; or the 7-5-4-3 in the hand 8-7-5-4-3, a rough 8. Smooth hands have greater possibilities of winning than their rough counterparts and should be played more aggressively.

If you make an 8-high hand or a smooth 9 on fifth street, you're in a strong position. You should bet and raise forcefully against players still holding drawing hands. You're the favorite, so you want to either force them out of the pot or make them pay for every card they try to catch.

Also play aggressively against weak players when you've got the goods. They'll stay in too long with inferior hands. Why not make your winning pot that much larger?

SEVEN-CARD STUD HIGH-LOW SPLIT STRATEGY

Seven-card high-low stud at the WSOP is played with a *qualifier*, a requirement that a player must have five unpaired cards of 8 or lower to win the low end of the pot. If no player has an 8-or-better qualifier, then the best high hand will win the entire pot. For example, if the best low at the table is 9-6-5-4-2, there is no qualified low hand and the best high hand will win the entire pot. This version of seven-card stud low is called *seven-card stud high-low split 8-or-better*. Splitting the pot into two parts, half for the best high hand and half for the best low, makes for an action-packed and exciting game.

Although you can win with either the best high hand or the best low hand, do not allow that to tempt you into playing too many hands. The same winning principle applies as in all poker games: Enter the betting only with good starting cards that have a good chance of winning. Staying in pots with hands that hold both high and low possibilities, but are mediocre in both directions, is a costly and weak strategy. Look for hands that give you possibilities of winning *both* the high and the low end of the pot. The problem with playing one-way hands in high-low is that your bets immediately lose half their value because you're going after only 50 percent of the pot. If you get shut out, you lose all your chips. And if you win, you only get half of the action.

And what if you happen to get caught in a pot where one player has a lock on one part of the pot? You're going to get whipsawed for a lot of bets, making your pursuit of 50 percent of the action very costly if you're the player getting trapped, especially if you're drawing dead. The math is not favorable for you in many one-way pots. So, when you are playing for one-half of the pot, you need your cards to be very strong.

The best starting hand in seven-card high-low stud is three suited cards 8 or below, particularly if one of these cards is an ace or you have three consecutive cards for a three-card straight flush. You have a great hand with excellent high and low potential and want to build the pot. If you're first in the pot, you should raise to build it up, but if you have raisers before you, just call.

Another big hand is three of a kind, especially if the trips are low. This is a very deceptive hand. A pair of aces with an 8 or lower to go with it, giving it two-way potential, is a strong hand as well. Other big pairs such as kings and queens, are almost worthless against an aggressive ace, as their scooping potential is limited and their high potential is vulnerable. In 8-or-better, big pairs take on more value because if low hands don't qualify, the high hand scoops the pot. However, you should never play a high hand that is not shaping up to be the best hand. This is an extremely important concept in hi-low, with or without the qualifier.

Other strong two-way starting hands are three-straights 8 or less (A-2-3, 2-3-4, 3-4-5, 4-5-6, 5-6-7, and 6-7-8), three straights 8 or lower with just one gap (such as 4-5-7 or 2-3-5), and three cards 8 or lower that include an ace (such as A-4-5, A-3-8, and A-3-5). You can play these hands strong on third street, raising or handling a few bets before your position. You have a great shot at low, and if your ace pairs and there is no other ace on board, you have a good shot at the high as well.

Even if you don't pair, sometimes the ace by itself might be enough to win the high. For example, a player holding K-Q-K would have to consider folding against your ace if you bet aggressively since his one-way high hand is looking at a possible bigger pair.

If your three-straight 8 or less has two gaps and doesn't include an ace, such 4-6-8 and 2-4-6, it has some value but should be folded against heavy betting. If, on fourth street, you're sitting with a four-card low topped by 8-7 or 8-6, you can't handle any action if another player looks like he's going for low as well—say by showing a 5-3 or 6-5 on board. And remember, an 8-led low hand is vulnerable against other players going low, particularly if you see no eights on their board.

Avoid playing middle pairs without high kickers, three-flushes that don't have three cards 8 or lower, three-straights with high cards (no scoop potential and only a draw to a high hand), and random cards that don't fit in with the starting hands discussed above. One important concept to keep in mind is that high hands can't turn into low hands, but low hands can turn into high ones if the right cards are drawn.

The nature of high-low stud calls for aggressive play. When you have a chance to scoop the pot or you have a lock on either the high or low end of the pot, bet forcefully. You want to create big pots and make the winnings that much juicier.

MIXED GAME TOURNAMENTS AT THE WSOP

The introduction of the $50,000 H.O.R.S.E championship event in 2006, won by Chip Reese, generated a lot of excitement, especially among professional players, many of whom consider it their championship event. More WSOP H.O.R.S.E tournaments have been added since then, so players who might not want to pony up five dimes can compete at more affordable levels.

H.O.R.S.E combines five games—limit hold'em, Omaha 8-or-better, razz, seven-card stud high, and seven-card stud high-low split 8-or-better—with levels rotating among the five variations every eight hands. All H.O.R.S.E events will be played as limit.

An exciting new entry to the palette of WSOP events is the new mixed-game format for tournaments. In contrast to the five-game H.O.R.S.E. events, the mixed-game tournaments combine *eight* different poker games: deuce-to-seven triple draw lowball, limit hold'em, Omaha high-low 8-or-better, razz, seven-card stud (high), pot-limit high, seven-card stud high-low split 8-or-better, and no-limit hold'em.

To excel in the H.O.R.S.E. and mixed games tournaments, you need to be an all-around player who is well versed in the strategies of the different games.

OTHER COMBINATION EVENTS

There are multiple events featuring combinations of games, such as limit/no-limit hold'em tournaments and Omaha/seven-card stud 8-or-better, which allow specialists of the two games to challenge their opponents for supremacy in those mixes. The combo tournaments rotate by number of hands or by time intervals (every half hour, for example).

BASIC STRATEGY FOR WINNING A WSOP TOURNAMENT

This is the big one, the tournament every poker player dreams of winning. Fame and fortune await the skillful and lucky player who goes all the way. It could be you this year, but to get to the promised land, you have to give luck every opportunity to come your way.

The first thing you must realize is that the Main Event is different. And not just because it's the big one. It's a deep stack tournament, which

Chris Ferguson
2000 World Champion of Poker

means that you start with a lot of chips and have ample time to make your moves. Therein lies your first directive: Take it slow. You have all the time in the world—at least, many hours—to wait for hands and situations you like. Unlike some of the smaller buy-in tournaments, where if you don't dance quickly, you'll be blinded away, the Main Event gives you plenty of opportunities to make moves.

The second thing to keep in mind is not to blow all your chips on a second-best hand. There is no need to push all your chips out there on an impulsive hunch. Sure, you may take down some chips, but if you unluckily run up against a monster hand, you're gone and there's no coming back—at least not until next year. And maybe it wasn't that you were unlucky—maybe you made some foolish mistakes.

Patience is the key. You've just invested $10,000 for the dream. Are you going to let it go that cheaply? Sometimes, even if you think your opponent is bluffing, you're better off not getting involved deeply in a hand that you don't really need to play. Better to lose a few chips that won't hurt you, than a lot of chips that will. In the Main Event, you'll have plenty of opportunities to find better places to take a stand.

Not many players start their tournament careers by playing the Main Event. Most people at the WSOP begin by playing a smaller tournament. The following tips will help you win any tournament your play.

PLAYING SHORT-STACKED

In almost every tournament you'll ever play, there will come a time—and that time may be practically the entire tournament—where you're going to be short-stacked and under a lot of pressure. The key to surviving with a short stack is staying calm. Don't give up. This does not mean that you can sit on your nest hatching eggs. As a short stack, you cannot afford to do that.

It does mean that you should carefully choose situations where you make a stand. Wait patiently before committing all your chips to a pot that may be your goodbye hand. If you still have chips, no matter how tiny your stack, it can grow quickly. All it takes is a few double ups, then another double up, and before you know it, you're a player with real chips, maybe even one of the chip leaders. It can happen fast, and it often does. The key is that you must still be in action at the table, ready for luck to find you.

GETTING IN THE MONEY

Tournaments become more exciting as the field narrows and you get close to the money table. You have fifty players to go, then forty, then twenty. Suddenly, only ten more players need to be knocked out and you will be cashing at the World Series of Poker! Not only is that prestigious and a great accomplishment, it also means you've finished in the top 10 percent of all players. You've won money and that's sweet. Bragging rights go with the territory. And there is one more thing it means: You have a legitimate chance, a real shot at getting to the final table.

But let's slow down for a second; first you have to get in the money. How do you achieve that?

First, if you're short-stacked and the blinds are eating you up, you have a tough decision to make. Do you go for it with an all-in move, or do you hold off and wait for enough players to bust out so that you assure yourself of cashing? If you can hang tight, and making the money is only a few hands away, why not wait and take the money? But if it looks like it will be awhile before the money hits, you're better off to make your move earlier if a strong opportunity presents itself.

You've got to get your chips in the middle eventually, so you're better off with a good situation than a bad one. If you lose, you're out, and that's okay. But if you win the hand, you can coast. Or if it suits your goals, you can get aggressive and try to accumulate chips.

That brings us to the bigger stack situations. If you have a decent sized stack or even a big stack, you can bully the short stacks that are hanging on for dear life. You're thinking ahead, you're thinking final table, and the more chips you have, the better your chances of getting there. If you win enough chips here, you can position yourself for a good run at the big money. Short stacks will not want to tangle with you when they're so close, nor will medium stacks that don't need to take chances.

With your bigger stack, you can take them out and end their dream—without them cashing—so they're unlikely to get in your way.

However you play, your strategy will be based on your goals. Are you trying to cash first, and worry about winning the whole enchilada later? Or is it "damn the torpedoes, full speed ahead"? Or possibly, "Let the chips fall where they may, I'm going for it now!" You decide. If you make the right decisions, and luck gives you a bit of a push, you get to the final table.

And that's where we pick up this discussion in the next part.

HELP! I MADE A FINAL TABLE!

Making a World Series of Poker final table is the experience of a lifetime. So few people ever get to be there—sitting under

Joe Hachem
2005 Main Event Champion

the lights, competing for the most coveted prize in poker, and hundreds of thousands, if not millions, of dollars! With the trials and tribulations of making it behind you, you now must face a whole new set of problems.

How do you handle the pressure? Do you play for the title or inch up the payout structure? How do you

handle the media and potential sponsorship opportunities? Most importantly, what strategies give you the best chance of taking home a bracelet?

Read on.

PREPARE YOURSELF FOR A MARATHON

Most final tables begin at 2 p.m. or 3 p.m. This is good. Sleep may not come easy the night before. You're anxious, you're nervous, you're excited. Fame, fortune, ego, respect—

so much is at stake. Try your best to get a full night's rest, and give yourself the opportunity to properly prepare for going all the way. Your only job prior to play is to do everything you can to turn your anxiety into focused energy. Here are some techniques that pros recommend to calm the nerves and prepare for your final table:

Yoga: Many professional poker players practice yoga on a regular basis. Las Vegas has plenty of yoga studios and many run classes all day. Yoga is great for bringing your mind clarity and focus, and your body a reprieve from sitting in a chair all day. Exercise: Your hotel probably has a workout facility and if not, most gyms will give you a day pass to try out the facility. Working in some cardio and getting your blood pumping will contribute vital energy that you will need throughout the day.

Spa/Massage: You've already locked up some pretty good money, so relax your mind and body with a massage or trip to the spa. You've been sitting for a few days and have a long day ahead of you, and a massage is an excellent way to help you get through it.

Meditation: Very few things are more effective than meditation for bringing in the calm. Just find a quiet spot where you can be alone and breathe deeply for at least ten minutes. Let your mind rest as you visualize what it will look like and how it will feel to win a WSOP bracelet.

Try to eat a healthy, light breakfast or lunch. Surround yourself with positive, encouraging people. You may want to avoid watching the news or reading the newspaper to keep stressful thoughts out of your head. Hop online to see if you can find any information on your opponents. Before your final table begins, a quick call to your family or home game crew will give you that last boost of confidence.

Now you're ready to sit down and get to work.

Play Solid Final Table Strategy

No advice is applicable to everyone in every situation, and certainly not for every player at a WSOP final table. Most final tables feature a mix of amateurs, semi-professionals and professionals, many with different agendas and goals. While it's safe to assume that almost everyone at the table wants to win the gold bracelet, still it means little to some players for whom cash is king. For others, creeping one spot up the money ladder means paying the mortgage for a few months, or putting their child through college. And for others, anything short of winning the bracelet means utter failure.

What Type of Player Are You?

Determine what type of player you are. Be honest with yourself. The bracelet is all that matters to many people. If you're this type of player, there really is no one strategy to employ. Continue to play the way you've been playing and hope that the skills and luck that have gotten you this far will carry you home. Remember, you don't have to bust everyone at the table to win the bracelet. Trying to do that often results in playing far too many pots, which usually is disastrous.

Be aware of your stack size relative to the rest of the field and the blinds, and use that information to help guide your decisions.

If you are the college-saving, mortgage-paying type, a very tight, let-everyone-else-bust-out style of play is a strong option; ' that is, if your stack size is large enough to allow you to sit back and play conservatively. Pay jumps are largest near the top, particularly in the top two spots, but you can earn significant extra money by hanging on for a while and letting other players battle it out.

Let's say that you fold nearly every hand for the first hour and two players bust out. In 7th place, you just increased your winnings by 90 percent over 9th place—and have paid for a college education, $75,084. As you can see, waiting out a few eliminations can really pad the bankroll. It can also do wonders for calming your nerves and getting you into your groove.

After a few early bust-outs, maybe your patience is rewarded with a big hand. Then you can decide whether you want to sit back a bit longer, or start playing a more aggressive style. The danger of playing conservatively, particularly if you start the final table with a short or medium size stack, is that while you are sitting back, the blinds and the blind stealers are eating up your chips. Your opponents at the final table will recognize what you're doing and mercilessly prey on your chips. If you choose this style, make sure you enter pots with the goods and play the pots you do enter aggressively.

Check out the final table payouts of the first $1,500 buy-in no-limit hold'em tournament, which attracted 3,929 players at the 2008 World Series of Poker. The structure of the payouts is likely to change at each year's WSOP, but you get the picture.

2008 WSOP $1,500 NO-LIMIT HOLD'EM FINAL TABLE PAYOUTS				
PLACE	PLAYER	$ AMOUNT	$ INCREASE	% INCREASE FROM SPOT BELOW
1	Grant Hinkle	$831,462	$311,243	59%
2	James Akenhead	$520,219	$131,932	33%
3	Chris Ferguson	$388,287	$61,139	18%
4	Theo Tran	$327,148	$58,994	22%
5	Mike Ngo	$268,154	$56,313	26%
6	Aaron Coulthard	$211,841	$53,630	33%
7	Melvin Jones	$158,211	$40,224	25%
8	David Bach	$117,987	$34,860	41%
9	Joe Rutledge	$83,127	$31,106*	37%*

*10th - 12th places paid $52,021.

Understand the Playing Style of the Big Stacks

Be aware of the tendencies of the big stacks. Many players who enter the final table with a big stack will sit back for a while and only get involved if they have to. This makes them prime targets for stealing the all-important blinds, which are your lifeblood as your stack dwindles. Don't let your stack get so short that it's easy for a big stack to look you up cheaply. If you get too short, you will be forced to pick a hand, throw in your chips, and cross your fingers—but that's the chance you take by playing a passive final-table style.

The blinds jump significantly at each level at the final table, so if you are fortunate enough to have a big stack, don't take it for granted. A few loose plays and a blind increase and you're not so big anymore. If you're the short stack, be sure that you have enough chips to ensure that your all-in bet has fold equity—that is, your bet is expensive enough so that a larger stack does not consider it a trivial call. In other words, don't wait too long to make your move. Get an understanding of how the rest of the table is playing and exploit both the super-aggressive players and the passive, move-up-the-pay-scale type of opponents.

Play Smarter as it Gets Later

As the event gets down to four or five players, the play usually loosens up significantly. Short stacks are desperate and looking for their last chance to make a meaningful double up. If you have a big stack, be careful about overcommitting. While the hand values for the lesser stacks will be weaker, your chips are too important at this point in the tournament to unnecessarily put them at risk. You don't get extra cash for being the one that busts the most players. The top money goes to the top finishers, however they get there. Play smart and you'll soon find yourself heads-up, money and bracelet sitting on the table, playing for a piece of poker history.

When you get heads-up, you will usually be granted a short break. Take advantage of it. Take a walk, get a drink, call your family, splash cool water on your face. Do what you have to do to prepare for what could be a long battle that lasts several hours. Winning heads-up play depends heavily on psychology, so focus intently on how you've seen your opponent play and act up to this point. Sitting back and waiting for hands isn't much of an option. Use your opponent's tendencies against him or her, and take down pots with well-timed raises, reraises and all-ins.

When that last river card falls on the felt and you take your first breath as a World Series of Poker Champion, remember to acknowledge your opponent. He or she has just gone through the same ordeal as you, but fate happened to be with you this night.

Now, smile pretty for the cameras…

MEETING WITH THE MEDIA

You will most likely be approached by the media prior to the start of your final table. If you like the idea of doing interviews, get to the Rio a bit early and they will find you. If you want to avoid the media, don't come into the tournament room until just before play begins, or politely decline their requests.

There are a large number of media outlets at the WSOP, and most will want hear what you have to say. You are under no obligation to speak to them, although it is a great opportunity to create a living record of your accomplishment at the World Series of Poker. Play it on repeat at your home game for some fun and, perhaps, an edge on your friends. It's your fifteen minutes of fame, we encourage you to soak it up!"

If you are unsure of your interview skills, follow these three simple tips:

1. Look at the interviewer as though you were having a conversation without the camera there. Many people try to alternate their glances between the camera and the interviewer, and it just ends up looking awkward. The time to play to the camera is at the end of the interview when you're saying goodbye.

2. Take a moment to think about your answer before you respond to the posed question. An editor can cut out pauses but can't paste in something you wish you had said.

3. If you mess up or don't like the answer you gave, ask the interviewer to stop and repeat the question. The pros do it, so can you!

Enjoy your time in the limelight!

DEALING WITH SPONSORS AND AGENTS

During the WSOP, you may be approached to wear a sponsor's logo patch during play (be sure to familiarize yourself with our rules on player apparel first). The WSOP doesn't acknowledge or endorse agents and everyone is free to negotiate for themselves. Winning a WSOP gold bracelet is sure to make you a marketable player afterwards as well, so don't feel pressured or time-constrained. Most sponsorship deals are structured such that the higher you place at the final table, the more you get paid. They can also be tiered based on your chip stack going into the final table. Typical deals pay a certain amount for ninth through fourth places, and increase with each subsequent position for the top three spots. It is sometimes difficult to land a sponsorship on your own, as sponsors often elect to work through agents to ensure efficiency and standardized terms as much as possible.

If you choose to work through an agent, you will have to sign an agreement that you should read carefully. If possible, you should interview several agents before making your selection. Select the agent you are most comfortable with, one who gives you the best service for what you are paying. Or, decline and trust the skills that got you to a good position in the tournament in the first place.

 **RESOURCES AT THE WSOP**

Congratulations! You've weathered the storm of bad beats, coin flips and cracked aces and cashed in a World Series of Poker event. Now what? Unless you're the one holding up a shiny new gold bracelet for the cameras, your first question is probably "Where's my money?"
Here's the scoop.

CASHING OUT

A tournament official will be standing by watching your final hand, and will lead you through the first steps of getting the prize money you've earned. The staff member will verify your photo ID and enter your name and Total Rewards card number into the system. At that point, you can leave if you don't want to stick around for the next part of the process. You can return to the payout room at your convenience, be it hours or weeks later.

To collect your winnings, you must visit the payout room located in the Palma room across from the player entrance to the Amazon room. You will need your Photo ID and Total Rewards card. The cashier will ask how you wish to receive your winnings. You can ask for cash or casino chips, complete a wire transfer, or put the funds on deposit at the main cage. Any combination of these methods is also possible.

You are solely responsible for your tax liability. Here are the guidelines the World Series of Poker follows:

U.S. Residents

If you are a U.S. citizen and resident and have winnings in excess of $5,000 net of the buy-in, you must fill out IRS form W-2G. You must provide your ID and social security number. If you do not know or are unwilling to give your social security number, 28 percent of your gross winnings will be withheld.

Non-U.S. Residents

If you are a non-U.S. resident and have winnings in excess of $5,000 net of the buy-in, you must fill out form 1042-S. As a foreign resident of a tax treaty country, you will also fill out form W8BEN if you have an ITIN (Individual Taxpayer Identification Number), or form W7 if you do not have an ITIN. The IRS issues ITINs to foreign nationals and others who have federal tax reporting or filing requirements and do not qualify for Social Security numbers. A non-resident alien individual not eligible for a SSN, who is required to file a U.S. tax return only to claim a refund of tax under the provisions of a U.S. tax treaty, needs an ITIN.

The World Series of Poker is required to withhold 30 percent of all taxable winnings from money winners who are from tax-treaty countries unless they have an ITIN. If you are from a non-tax treaty country, 30 percent of all taxable winnings will be withheld with or without an ITIN.

Tax-Treaty Countries

Austria, Belgium, Bulgaria, Czech Republic, Denmark, Finland, France, Germany, Hungary, Ireland, Iceland, Italy, Japan, Latvia, Lithuania, Luxembourg, Netherlands, Russian Federation, Slovak Republic, Slovenia, South Africa, Spain, Sweden, Tunisia, Turkey, Ukraine and the United Kingdom. For more information on ITINs visit: www.irs.gov/individuals/

article/0,,id=96287,00.html#what. Once you complete the paperwork, you'll soon be out the door with a pocketful of cash.

Tipping

Should you tip when you make a big cashout? There are two schools of thought on this. Some pros feel that tipping is unnecessary because money has already been removed from the prize pool for this purpose, while others feel that an extra gratuity is appropriate.

If you would like to tip for good service performed, a standard range is 1-2 percent of your payout—though, of course, any amount you'd like to leave is up to you. You mark your tip on the payout receipt you'll be given right after busting out. This is the form you'll take to the cashier's cage to get your prize money. Note that the tips get divided among all tournament staff, including the dealers and floor staff.

WIRE TRANSFER AND CASHIER'S CHECK INSTRUCTIONS

WIRE INSTRUCTIONS

Fax your **wire transfer confirmation** along with completed **Pre-Registration Form** to 702-856-3463.
Attention: WSOP

Wire Information:

ABA/Routing Number: 026009593
Swift: Bofaus3n
Bank Name: Bank Of America
Bank Address: 300 South 4th Street, Las Vegas, Nevada 89101
Beneficiary: Harrah's Interactive Entertainment, Inc.
Account Number: 004969442145
Special Instructions: Ref 1: Player Name
Ref 2: WSOP Event Number

The "Special Instructions" area is standard to any domestic and international bank, where the customer can request the bank to be more specific when sending this wire transfer. This space will only accommodate 25-35 characters on each line. Third-Party payments will not be accepted unless approved by corporate sponsorship and licensing. Otherwise, Player Name must match remitter name.

International Wires: Please be aware that all transaction fees are the responsibility of the sender. This includes all fees charged by correspondent banks. Wires received with fees deducted from the buy-in amount will require an additional deposit to complete registration. WSOP will make one attempt to contact the remitter via email to notify of payment shortage. Pre-Registration payments that are short will not be confirmed until complete payment has been received.

Payment is a deposit only. You must complete registration at The Rio, Las Vegas, NV for the events as set forth in the rules available at www.worldseriesofpoker.com. Your deposit may be applied to event registration at that time or for any other use.

CASHIER'S CHECK INSTRUCTIONS
Please mail **Cashier's Check** along with completed **Pre-Registration Form** to:
Rio Properties, Inc,
DBA Rio All-Suite Hotel & Casino,
World Series of Poker
Attention: Accounting Office,
P O Box 14160,
Las Vegas, Nevada 89114-4160

Check Information
Payable To: World Series of Poker
Memo: Ref 1: Customer Name
Ref 2: WSOP Event Number

There will be no Third-Party registrations. Check remitter name must match player name. Payment is a deposit only. You must complete pre-registration at The Rio, Las Vegas, NV for the events as set forth in the rules available at www. worldseriesofpoker.com.

GENERAL WSOP INFORMATION

MAILING ADDRESS:

Rio All-Suite Hotel & Casino 3700 West Flamingo Road Las Vegas, NV 89103 (702) 777-7777 or (800) PLAY-RIO www.riolasvegas.com	World Series of Poker c/o Harrah's Entertainment One Caesars Palace Drive Las Vegas, NV. 89109 (702) 407-6000 www.worldseriesofpoker.com

WSOP TOURNAMENT LOCATION

The WSOP is held in the Rio Convention Center, one block west on Flamingo Road (off of Interstate 15). The Pavilion, Amazon, Brasilia and Miranda Ballrooms make up the majority of the tournament areas, with more than 300 poker tables in action for the WSOP.

KEY INFORMATION

For the most comprehensive information on the World Series of Poker, go to www.worldseriesofpoker.com

For room reservations, go to:
http://www.worldseriesofpoker.com/reservations/

For pre-registration of events, go to
http://www.worldseriesofpoker.com/registration/

For general questions about the WSOP,
email wsopissues@harrahs.com or
call 877-FOR-WSOP (877-367-9767)

RESTAURANTS

ALL-AMERICAN BAR & GRILLE
From crisp salads, sandwiches, fresh seafood and "Rio Dry Aged" Angus steaks, even the heartiest appetite will be satisfied at the All-American Bar & Grille. 702-777-7767. Open daily 11 a.m. to 6 a.m.

BUZIO'S SEAFOOD RESTAURANT
Seafood fresh from the docks and traditional New England fare. Offers outstanding views of the Rio's Ipanema Beach and swimming pools. 702-777-7697. Open Wednesday-Sunday 5 p.m to 11 p.m.

CARNIVAL WORLD BUFFET
From pizza to omelets, sushi to teppanyaki, fresh carved meats to Asian barbeque; the Carnival World Buffet offers distinct dining experiences from around the world featuring live-action cooking right before your eyes. 702-777-7757.

GAYLORD INDIAN RESTAURANT
Entree specialties include tandoori chicken, prawns and salmon, assorted meat kabobs, lamb curries, chicken curries and seafood delicacies. 702-777-2277. Open daily 5 p.m to 11 p.m, Friday-Sunday 11:30 a.m. to 2:30 p.m.

HAMADA'S ASIANA RESTAURANT
Choose from Japanese Teppanyaki table-side cooking and an exotic menu featuring traditional Japanese dishes including fresh sushi. 702-777-2770. Open daily from 5:30 p.m to 9:30 p.m.

MARTORANO'S
Italian-American cooking by hands-on chef Steve Martorano. Select from a variety of options including veal chops, pasta, fish and chicken. 702-777-7740. Open daily 6 p.m to 10:30 p.m.

SAO PAULO CAFE
Choose from a wide variety of traditional favorites. 702-777-2761. Open daily 6 a.m. to 9 p.m.

RUB BBQ

Just off the casino floor in the Masquerade Village, RUB BBQ features championship-level barbecue created by Paul Kirk. 702-777-7777. Open Monday-Tuesday 4 p.m to 11 p.m, Wednesday-Sunday 11 a.m. to 12 a.m.

VILLAGE SEAFOOD BUFFET

The refined Village Seafood Buffet is Las Vegas' only seafood buffet serving the freshest seafood from around the world, flown in daily with restaurant-style execution. 702-777-7943. Open Sunday-Thursday 4 p.m to 10 p.m, Friday-Saturday 3:30 p.m to 10:30 p.m.

VOODOO STEAK

Situated high above Las Vegas on the 50th floor of the Rio's Masquerade Tower, VooDoo Steak provides a breathtaking city view, gourmet steaks, and American cuisine with French Creole flair. 702-777-8090. Open daily 5 p.m to 11 p.m.

2010 WSOP OFFICIAL TOURNAMENT RULES

SECTION I – TOURNAMENT REGISTRATION AND ENTRY

1.   As used herein, "Rio" means Rio Properties, Inc. and its parent, affiliates and subsidiaries including, but not limited to, Rio Properties, Inc, dba Rio All-Suite Hotel & Casino. Rio reserves the right to refuse anyone entry into the Tournament, in its sole and absolute discretion.

2.   Entry into the World Series of Poker (herein "WSOP" refers to all events from May 27, 2010 through November 10, 2010) is limited to persons 21 years of age and older, with proof of age, that Rio, acting in its sole and absolute discretion, deems appropriate. Only one entry is allowed per person, per event as set forth in event descriptions.

3.   Participants may register for any scheduled 2010 WSOP Tournament event in person at the WSOP Registration Area in the Rio All-Suite Hotel & Casino, 3700 W. Flamingo Road, Las Vegas, Nevada 89103, or may pre-register for any scheduled 2010 WSOP Tournament event up to two weeks prior to an event's start date via the online method at www.wsop.com. Cash, cashier's checks drawn from accredited banks and made out to

registrants or the Rio, and Rio gaming chips may be used to pay for entry into a WSOP event.

4.   Subject to the restrictions described in these rules, pre-registrations can be initiated by downloading a pre-registration form online at www.wsop.com/registration/. The completed form and deposit must be submitted to the Rio no later than two weeks prior to the start of the selected event(s). The deposit required is the full amount of the event's entry fee. It may be applied to the event registration at the Rio or used for whatever other purpose a participant may elect. Pre-registration will close two weeks prior to the start of any particular event. Thereafter, participants may register in person at the Rio. All pre-registrants must finalize their registration on site. Complete instructions can be found at www.wsop.com. Pre-registered participants will need to present proof of identity (passport, driver's license, state or military identification card) in person at the Rio to complete the registration process and to obtain his or her table and seat assignment. Participants wishing to apply the deposit to an event other than what was selected during pre-registration must do so in person at the Rio.

5.   Third-party registrations for players are not permitted unless submitted by official WSOP sponsors; official WSOP promotional partners, or official WSOP product licensees. No third-party registrations will be accepted from online gaming sites conducting business with U.S. residents. For more information regarding third-party entries please contact Angele Marshall by email at anmarshall@harrahs.com.

6.   Rio may limit the number of entries into any WSOP event and may award entries into any event through any means it deems appropriate. Rio intends to award a limited number of entries through satellite Tournaments, third-party marketing arrangements and or other promotional activities in its sole and absolute discretion. Rio will add the required entry fee(s) to the prize pool.

7.   Participants are responsible for payment of any and all taxes, licenses, registrations and other fees associated with Tournament registration.

8.   Participants must show their current valid picture identification (driver's license, state or military identification card) acceptable to Rio at Registration and Will Call. If a participant is not a U.S. citizen, a current passport, consular identification or alien registration card is required.

9.   Players are required to obtain a Harrah's Total Reward's Card prior to registering for any WSOP Tournament or Satellite event. Total Rewards Card are available without payment of any kind at the Total Rewards Center at Rio or any of Rio's affiliates.

10.   Participants are responsible for checking their Tournament entry receipts before they leave the registration window. All changes must be made before the start of any event.

11   Registration is open until the end of the second level of any event. If there is a player break at the end of the second level, registration will remain upon until the Tournament resumes play.

12.   Late registrants for any event will be subject to the following rules in addition to all other rules. A late registrant is defined as a player that registers for an event after the Tournament has officially started. Any player registering for an event after all initial tables allocated for that tournament have been filled will begin play at the start of the subsequent level. All late registrants will start the Tournament with a full chip stack. In games with blinds, a player who enters during the first round of play will receive no penalty so long as the blinds have not passed their starting position. Players who enter after the first round of blinds must wait until their first opportunity to post to begin play. In games with only antes, the player must ante at their first opportunity. In mixed events such as HORSE, late entries after the first round of play must wait to post in blind games, and ante in stud games at their first opportunity.

13.   Any player registering for multiple events and who make Day Two or the final table of a particular event, may transfer his or her buy-in for the subsequent event to another event, or may also receive a refund, upon request, provided that the transfer or refund is approved and initiated prior to the beginning of the event from which a transfer or refund is being requested.

14.   Any player who has not taken a hand by the start of the third level will be considered a "no show." These players will have their chips removed from play and will not be eligible to participate in that event. The buy-ins for "no shows" will be removed from the prize pool and placed on safekeeping in that player's name at the Main WSOP Registration cage after the second level of play. All funds placed on safekeeping due to no shows must be claimed prior to July 17th, 2010. Funds not claimed on or before that date shall be forfeited to Rio and shall not be refunded for any reason whatsoever.

15.   Employees of Rio and its parent, subsidiaries, affiliates, owned, operated or managed properties, contractors hired for the operation of the WSOP or parent companies and immediate family members of such employees are not eligible to play in any WSOP events, unless approved in advance by Rio. Immediate Family is defined as: spouse, children and any relative or other person residing in the employee's place of residence.

HET Employees are allowed to participate in the Annual WSOP Casino Employee's Event with prior approval from their respective department.

16.   Individuals who are excluded from casino facilities, either through a government program or by their own request, are not eligible.

17.   Each participant must certify their own eligibility.

18.   No teams, substitutes, transfers or assisted play will be permitted. Rio reserves the right to accommodate players based on special needs.

19.   Cancellations or voids must be completed prior to the start of a particular event. Rio will issue refunds related to entry fees paid by authorized third-party registrants only to the third-party that paid Rio the registration fee. Please contact Poker Operations Manager, Andrew Rich, for a Cancellation Form at the WSOP Tournament Offices at the Rio, by email to arich@lvrio.harrahs.com, or by telephoning 702-777-6777. The Cancellation Form must be signed and received prior to the start of a particular event. Email notification is also acceptable provided such notification is received and approved by Rio prior to the start of the event.

20.   By submitting a Pre-Registration Form to Rio for registration in and/or participation in the WSOP, such persons and/or entities agree to these rules.

21.   The ability to pre-register as described in these rules is void where prohibited or in any way restricted by law.

22.   Entries will be retained for record-keeping purposes in accordance with local legal requirements.

SECTION II – TOURNAMENT SCHEDULING

23.   WSOP Tournament times are approximate. Rio reserves the right to change WSOP Tournament times in its sole and absolute discretion.

24.   Rio may cancel, modify, relocate or reschedule the WSOP or any individual event within the WSOP for any reason with prior notification to the appropriate gaming regulators, to the extent such is required.

25.   Rio is not responsible for electronic transmission errors or delays resulting in omission, interruption, deletion, defect, delay in operations or transmission, theft or destruction or unauthorized access to or alterations of entry materials, or for technical, hardware, software, or telephone failures of any kind, lost or unavailable connections, fraud, incomplete, garbled, or delayed computer transmissions, whether caused by Rio, users, or by any of the equipment or programming associated with or utilized in the promotion or by any technical or human error that may occur in the processing of submissions, any of which may limit, restrict, or prevent a participant's ability to participate in the Tournament.

26.   Rio is not responsible for injuries or losses arising or resulting from participation in the WSOP and is not liable for any acts or omissions by employees, whether negligent or willful, in the conduct of the WSOP, and is not liable in the event of any equipment or software malfunction. This includes, but is not limited to, any loss of any Tournament chips players leave at playing tables during Tournament play, except during authorized breaks.

27.   If for any reason the Tournament is not capable of running as planned, including infection by computer virus, bugs, tampering, unauthorized intervention, fraud, technical failures, or any other causes within or beyond the control of Rio that corrupt or affect the administration, security, fairness, integrity or proper conduct of this Tournament, Rio reserves the right at its sole discretion to cancel, terminate, modify or suspend the Tournament.

SECTION III – PRIZING AND SEATING

28.   Prizes and entries are non-transferable. Prize structures depend on the number of entrants and type of event.

29.   Winners are responsible for payment of any and all taxes, licenses, registrations and other fees associated with Tournament prizes.

30.   Winners must show their current valid picture identification (driver's license, state or military identification card) acceptable to Rio in order to collect prizes. If a participant is not a U.S. citizen, a current passport, consular identification or alien registration card is required.

31.   Entrants will be assigned to a table and seat through a random computer selection.

32.   A random seating draw for an event will be determined based on expected participation. Tournament management reserves the right to allow additional table seating beyond expected capacity. In the event tables are added to a Tournament beyond the anticipated random draw, those players assigned to the additional tables will be the first to break.

33.   If the participant is not present at the start of the Tournament, all forced antes and blinds bets will be removed from an absent player's stack accordingly. If player shows up and still has chips remaining, he or she may play his or her chips.

34.   Rio reserves the right to cancel, change or modify the WSOP at any time, for any reason, subject to all applicable regulatory approval, provided that such modification shall not, as of the date of such modification, materially alter or change any participant's prize already awarded.

35.   Non-value Tournament chips are used for the Tournament and are the exclusive property of Rio and may not be removed from the

Tournament area or the assigned event. Players found to be transferring chips from one event to another or from one player to another will be subject to penalty in accordance with Rule No. 37.

36.   WSOP Buy-In Chips are no cash value chips won by a Player in a Satellite Tournament conducted at Rio which may only be applied toward tournament buy-ins equal to or greater than $500 commencing on May 27th and concluding on July 17th, 2010. All WSOP Buy-In Chips will expire on July 17th, 2010 and will not be accepted at any future WSOP event or any other event at Rio or any of its affiliates.

SECTION IV – PLAYER CONDUCT AND TOURNAMENT INTEGRITY

37.

A.   The competitive integrity of all Tournament play at the World Series of Poker is paramount. All participants must adhere to the spirit and letter of the Official Rules of the WSOP which forbid play or any action that is illegal, unethical or constitutes cheating or collusion in any form.

  i.   Cheating is defined as any act a person engages in to break the established rules of play to gain an advantage.

  ii.   Cheating includes, but is not limited to, acts such as: collusion; chip stealing; transferring non-value Tournament chips from one event to another; card marking; card substitution; or the use of any kind of cheating device.

  iii.   Collusion is defined as any agreement amongst two (2) or more players to engage in illegal or unethical acts against other players.

  iv.   Collusion includes, but is not limited to, acts such as: chip dumping; soft play; sharing card information with another player; sending or receiving signals from or to another player; the use of electronic communication with the intent to facilitate collusion; and any other act that Rio and WSOP deem inappropriate.

B.   All participants are entitled to expect civility and courtesy from one another at every Tournament table and throughout the Tournament area. Any individual who encounters behavior that is not civil or courteous --or is abusive in any way --is encouraged to immediately contact a Tournament official. This shall include, but is not limited to, any player whose personal hygiene has become disruptive to the other players seated at their table. The determination as to whether an individual's personal hygiene is disruptive to other players shall be determined by the Tournament Staff which may, in its discretion, implement sanctions upon any such player who refuses to remedy the situation in a manner satisfactory to Rio.

C. Rio will penalize any act that, in the sole and absolute discretion of Rio, is inconsistent with the official rules or bests interests of the Tournament.

D. Anyone found to have engaged in or attempted to engage in any act that Tournament officials believe in their sole and absolute discretion compromises or could compromise the competitive integrity of the WSOP will be subject to sanctions imposed by Rio. The nature and extent of the sanctions imposed shall be in the sole and absolute discretion of Rio and may include, but shall not be limited to the following: · FORFEITURE OF CHIPS · FORFEITURE OF PRIZE MONEY · EJECTION FROM THE TOURNAMENT · LOSS OF PRIVILEGE TO PARTICIPATE IN FUTURE WSOP EVENTS · EXCLUSION FROM ENTERING THE PREMISES OF ALL DESIGNATED AFFILIATES OF RIO.

E. Any and all violations of this Code of Player Conduct may be publicly disclosed in an effort to deter future violations and to assist other poker Tournaments in identifying players who engage in play or any action that is illegal, unethical, or constitutes cheating or collusion in any form.

38. In addition to that authorized in Rule 37, Rio may impose penalties of any kind or nature upon any person who gives, makes, issues, authorizes or endorses any statement or action having, or designed to have, an effect prejudicial or detrimental to the best interest of the Tournament as determined by Rio, acting in its sole and absolute discretion. This may include, but shall not be limited to, expulsion from the event and property, forfeiture of a player's entry fee(s) and/or loss of the right to participate in this and/or any other Tournament conducted by Rio. Additionally, Rio may in its sole and absolute discretion impose penalties of any kind or nature upon any person who, in Rio view engages in inappropriate conduct during Tournament play.

39. Rio, in its sole and absolute discretion, may also disqualify any person from receiving any prize based upon fraud, dishonesty, violation of promotional rules or other misconduct while on the property, for acts otherwise occurring in relation to the World Series of Poker, or as otherwise reasonable or necessary for Rio to comply with applicable statutes and regulations. Rio also reserves the right to exclude any individual(s) acting

in a disruptive or inappropriate manner or counter to the best interests of the Tournament.

40.   Any attempt by any person to deliberately damage, corrupt or undermine the operation of the WSOP Tournament may be a violation of criminal and civil laws. Should such an attempt be made, Rio reserves the right to seek damages from any such person to the fullest extent of the law.

41.   All decisions regarding the interpretation of World Series of Poker Rules, player eligibility, scheduling and staging of the Tournament, and penalties for misconduct lie solely with Rio, whose decisions are final.

42.   Rio employees will use reasonable efforts to consider the best interests of the Tournament and fairness as the top priority in the decision-making process, with the understanding that "best interests of the Tournament and fairness" shall be determined by Rio, acting in its sole and absolute discretion. Unusual circumstances can, on occasion, dictate that the technical interpretation of the rules be balanced against the interest of fairness. Rio decisions are final and can not be appealed and shall not give rise to any claim for monetary damages, as each participant understands that, while poker is primarily and largely a game of skill, the outcome of any particular hand or event is dependent on many factors, including but not limited to the cards dealt, the cards retained and the actions of other participants.

43.   Rio prohibits the use of obscene or foul language in any public area of the casino at any time. Any player who uses such language or makes a foul, profane, obscene or vulgar statement, or speaks abusively or in an intimidating manner to another player, a dealer or a Tournament staff member, will be penalized. These penalties will be levied based on Rules 37, 92 and 96.

44.   Excessive celebration through extended theatrics, inappropriate behavior, or physical actions, gestures, or conduct will be subject to penalty. Any player that engages a member of the Tournament staff during the celebration or utilizes any property of Rio will be penalized in accordance with Rules No. 37, 92, and 96. Rio property includes but is not limited to chairs, Tournament tables, and stanchions.

45.   Player or staff abuse will not be tolerated. A player will incur a penalty up to and including disqualification for any abuse towards another player or staff member, and the player could be asked to leave the property. Repeated etiquette violations such as touching another player's cards or chips, delay of game and excessive chatter will result in penalties.

46. The WSOP is subject to all applicable federal, state, and local laws and regulations, including gaming, and all aspects of the WSOP are subject to the approval of appropriate regulatory authorities.

47. Tournament Rules and any and all changes in the rules and event descriptions for the WSOP May 27, 2010, through November 10, 2010 in Las Vegas, Nevada, will be available at the Tournament facilities in the Rio All-Suite Hotel & Casino as well as on the internet on the bottom of the home page of www.wsop.com.

48. Where a situation arises that is not covered by these rules, Rio shall have the sole authority to render a judgment, including the imposition of a penalty, in accordance with the best interests of the Tournament and the maintenance of its integrity and public confidence.

SECTION V – PLAYER LIKENESS AND IMAGE

49. Prior to entering and playing in the Tournament, each participant must execute a Player Release Form. Failure to do so may, at the option of Rio acting in its sole and absolute discretion, subject the player to immediate disqualification at any point in the Tournament. If the player is disqualified he or she shall forfeit all entry fees and not be entitled to any Tournament prize monies or any other prize consideration that he or she may have qualified for at the point of disqualification.

50. Tournament participants may wear apparel with multiple logos, patches or promotional language. However, no individual logo, patch or block of promotional language is to be larger than 12 square inches. Temporary tattoos, adhesive strips for the skin, and "band-aids" with logos or promotional language are not permitted at any time.

A. No single company name, brand, or affiliated and similar name or brand is to be represented more than once on any individual article of clothing.

B. During all events taped for television coverage:

   i. During all events taped for television coverage, and at the start of each television taping day, no more than three (3) players at the Final Table – and all other tables featured for television coverage – will be allowed to wear apparel with logos, patches or promotional language from the same entity.

   ii. Should there be more than three (3) players representing the same entity at the start of a televised Final or feature table – and those players can not agree which player will remove or cover their logos for the common entity – a WSOP official will draw high-card prior to the start of play to determine which players will be allowed to wear the logos of the common entity. After the draw of the high-card, the affected player(s) must either cover the relevant logo(s) or change their apparel.

iii. Under no circumstance may players seated at televised Final or Feature add logos, patches or promotional language to their apparel after the beginning of that day's session of play.

C. Under no circumstances will any logo, slogan or promotional language be permitted that Rio, acting in its sole discretion, determines:

i. Contains any false, unsubstantiated, or unwarranted claims for any product or service, or make any testimonials that Rio, in its sole and absolute discretion, considers unethical;

ii. Advertises any non-prescription or non "over the counter" drug, tobacco product, handgun or handgun ammunition;

iii. Contains any material constituting or relating to a lottery, a contest of any kind in which the public is unfairly treated or any enterprise, service or product that abets, assists or promotes illegal gambling;

iv. Contains any material that is defamatory, obscene, profane, vulgar, repulsive or offensive, either in theme or in treatment or that describes or depicts repellently any internal bodily functions or symptomatic results of internal conditions, or refers to matters that are not considered socially acceptable topics;

v. Advertises any pornographic products;

vi. Includes any element of intellectual property without the owner's consent to such use or that may give rise to any claim of infringement, misappropriation, or other form of unfair competition;

vii. Disparages or libels any person or product;

viii. Advertises any online gaming site that conducts business with U.S. residents;

ix. Are or might be injurious or prejudicial to the interests of the WSOP or Rio or is otherwise contrary to honest advertising and reputable business in general. This includes but is not limited to the name or logo of any person or entity that uses or has used the trademarks, trade names or logos of Rio or its affiliated companies without written authorization from an authorized officer of Rio;

x. In addition, all logos, patches, and promotional language for any dot.net website must contain a clear and visible "dot.net" suffix at least the same size as the site name;

xi. Rio reserves the right at all times to impose a ban on any apparel deemed objectionable by Rio, in its sole and absolute discretion.

D. The WSOP reserves the right to refuse entry or continued participation in an event to any player who does not comply with the aforementioned apparel rules

51. Players may not cover or conceal their facial identity. Tournament officials must be able to distinguish the identity of each player at all times and may instruct players to remove any material that inhibits their identification or is a distraction to other players or tournament officials. Players may wear sunglasses and sweat shirts with hoods, but may be asked to remove them if they cannot be identified by tournament officials.

SECTION VI – POKER RULES

52. The Tournament Director, Managers, and Supervisors are to consider the best interest of the game and fairness as the top priority in the decision-making process. Unusual circumstances can on occasion dictate that decisions in the interest of fairness take priority over the technical rules. The Tournament Director reserves the right to overrule any floor decision.

53. Rio reserves the right to cancel or alter any event at its sole discretion in the best interest of the casino or its players.

54. The English-only rule will be enforced at all WSOP tables during Tournament play. Players who violate this rule are subject to penalty in accordance with Rule No. 92.

55. Cell Phone Rule: All cell phones and other voice-enabled and "ringing" electronic devices must be turned off during tournament play. Players not involved in a hand (cards in muck) shall be permitted to text/email at the table, but shall not be permitted to text/email any other player at the table. If Rio, acting in its sole and absolute discretion, believes a player is communicating with another player at the table, both parties will be immediately disqualified from the tournament and face imposition of additional penalties as described in Rule 37. All players desiring to talk on a cell phone must be at least one table length away from their assigned table during all said communication. Those individuals who talk on a cell phone not at least one table length away from their assigned table shall be subject to a penalty to be determined by Tournament Staff. No cell phones or other electronic communication device can be placed on a poker table.

56.   Approved Electronic Device Rule: Players are allowed to use as approved electronic devices iPods, MP3 and other music players or noise-reduction headsets during Tournament play until they have reached the money in any Tournament, so long as the approved electronic devices are not used to collude or cheat in any way. Once players are in the money in any Tournament, all approved electronic devices must be removed. An announcement will be made to players once they have reached the money to remove all such electronic devices. Failure to do so will results in a penalty up to and including disqualification, in accordance with Rule 92.

57.   Tournament and satellite seats will be randomly assigned. Tournament staff reserves the right to relocate players from their assigned seat to accommodate players based on special needs, and to balance tables at the start of the Tournament.

58.   The breaking order for an event will be posted at the close of registration for that event. The table to which a player is moved will be specified by a predetermined procedure. Players going from a broken table to fill in seats assume the rights and responsibilities of the position. They can get the big blind, the small blind or the button. The only place they cannot get a hand is between the small blind and the button. Rio reserves the right to alter the breaking order due to unusual circumstances.

59.   Play will halt at any table that is at least three players short. In fields greater than 20 tables, players will be moved from the next numerical table at full capacity to the short table. Once a Tournament is below 20 tables, players will be moved from the next table in the breaking order that is at full capacity to the short table. Players moving from a full table to a short table assume the same rights and responsibilities of the position as outlined in Rule No. 58.

A.   In flop and mixed games, players will be moved from the big blind to the worst position, including taking a single big blind. Worst position is never the small blind. In stud only games, players will be moved by position (the last seat to open up at the short table is the seat to be filled).

B.   When the Tournament reaches 12 tables, the remaining tables will be balanced within 1 player until the final table is reached. There will be a re-draw for seat assignments when play reaches 3 tables, again at 2 tables, and for the final table seat assignments for events that have 100 or more participants. For events with less than 100 participants but more than 50, there will be a re-draw at 2 tables and again for final table seat assignments.

60.   Cards speak. Verbal declarations as to the content of a player's hand are not binding; however at Rio discretion, any player deliberately miscalling his hand will be subject to penalty in accordance with Rule No. 92.

61.   All cards will be turned face up once a player is all in and all action is complete. If a player accidentally folds/mucks their hand before cards are turned up, the Tournament Staff reserves the right to retrieve the folded/mucked cards if the cards are clearly identifiable.

62.   A dealer cannot kill a winning hand that was tabled and was obviously the winning hand. Players are encouraged to assist in reading tabled hands if it appears that an error is about to be made.

63.   At the end of the last round of betting, the player who made the last aggressive betting action in that betting round must show first. If there was no bet during the final round, the player to the left of the button shows first, and so on in a clockwise direction. In stud games, the player with the high board must show first. In razz, the lowest board shows first. At showdown, any player at the table may request to see a folded hand from any player who has called all bets on the last round of betting. If a player with the last aggressive action on the last round of betting refuses to show their hand and intentionally mucks his or her hand, the player in violation will receive a penalty, in accordance with Rule No. 92.

64.   Odd Chips: The odd chip(s) will go to the high hand. In flop games, when there are two (2) or more high hands or two (2) or more low hands, the odd chip(s) will go to the left of the button. In stud-type games, the odd chip will go to the high card by suit. However, when hands have identical value, e.g., a wheel in Omaha 8 or Better, the pot will be split as evenly as possible. In Omaha/Stud 8 or Better, the pot will be split down to the lowest denomination chip in play. If an odd chip exists as a result from the first split of a pot, it will be awarded to the high hand. If an additional odd chip results from the split of the low hands, it will be awarded to the player in the worse position.

65.   Each side pot will be split as a separate pot. Pots will not be mixed together before they are split.

66.   A player must show both of his or her cards when playing the board to get part of the pot.

67.   The right to dispute a hand ends when a new hand begins. A hand begins with the first riffle.

68.   Chip race rule: Race-off is defined as removal of a denomination chip no longer in use. When it is time to color-up chips, they will be raced off with a maximum of one chip going to any player. The chip race will

always start at the first player left of the dealer. A player cannot be raced out of a Tournament. In the event that a player has only one chip remaining, the regular race procedure will take place. If that player loses the race, he or she will be given one chip of the smallest denomination still in play. Players found to have lower denomination chips remaining in their stack after the race-off will forfeit those chips unless they are equivalent in value to a chip still in play. Players are encouraged to witness the chip race.

69.   Deck changes will be on the dealer push or limit changes or as prescribed by Rio. Players may not ask for deck changes unless a card is damaged.

70.   When time has elapsed in a round and a new round is announced by a member of the Tournament staff, the new limits apply to the next hand. As stated in Rule No. 67, a new hand begins with the first riffle.

71.   Calling-for-clock procedures: Once a reasonable amount of time, which is no less than two minutes, has passed and a clock is called, a player will be given one (1) minute to act. If action has not been taken by the time the minute has expired, there will be a ten (10) second countdown. If a player has not acted on his hand by the time the countdown is over, the hand will be dead. Tournament Supervisors reserve the right to speed up the amount of time allotted for a clock if it appears that a player is deliberately stalling. Any player intentionally stalling the progress of the game will incur a penalty in accordance with Rule No. 92.

72.   In cases where hands are concluded prior to the last card being dealt, the next card to be dealt will not be exposed under any circumstances. This prohibited practice is commonly referred to as "rabbit hunting."

73.   A player must be at his or her seat by the time all players have been dealt complete initial hands to have a live hand. Players must be at their seats to call time. "At your seat" is defined as being within reach or touch of your chair.

74.   Players must remain at the table if they still have action pending on a live hand. If a player leaves the table before they have acted on their hand, a penalty, in accordance with Rule No. 92, will be enforced when the player in violation returns to the table.

75.   Tournament play will use the dead button rule. Dead Button is defined as a button that cannot be advanced due to elimination of a player or the seating of a new player into a position between the small blind and the button.

76.   A player who intentionally dodges his or her blind(s) when moving from a broken table must forfeit both blinds and incur a penalty, in accordance with Rule No. 92.

77.   When heads up in blind games, the small blind is on the button and acts first. When beginning heads-up play, the button may need to be adjusted to ensure no player takes the big blind twice.

78.   In stud-type games, if any of the players' two down cards are exposed due to a dealer error, it is a misdeal. In flop games, exposure of one of the first two cards dealt is a misdeal. Players may be dealt two consecutive cards on the button. The following situations may also be cause for a misdeal, if during the initial deal:

    a)   two or more extra cards have been dealt

    b)   the first card was dealt to the wrong position

    c)   cards have been dealt to an empty seat or a player not entitled to a hand or

    d)   a player has been dealt out who is entitled to a hand provided substantial action has not occurred. Substantial action is considered: three folds, three checks, two or more calls, a fold and a call, or a bet and or a raise or a call and or a fold.

79.   If the flop contains four (rather than three) cards, whether exposed or not, the dealer shall scramble the four cards face down. A tournament official will be called to randomly select one card to be used as the next burn card and the remaining three cards will become the flop.

80.   Verbal declarations in turn regarding wagers are binding. Players must act in turn at all times. Action out of turn will be binding if the action to that player has not changed. A check, call or fold is not considered action changing. If a player acts out of turn and the action changes, the person who acted out of turn may change their action by calling, raising or folding and may have their chips returned. Players may not intentionally act out of turn to influence play before them. Violators will receive a penalty in accordance with Rule No. 92.

81.   All chips put into the pot in turn stay in the pot. If a player has raised and his or her hand is killed before the raise is called, the player may be entitled to the raise back, but will forfeit the amount of the call. Any chips put into the pot out of turn fall under the action "may or may not be binding" Rule No. 80.

82.   In no-limit or pot-limit, a raise must be made by

    a.)   Placing the full amount in the pot in one or more continuous motion(s) without going back toward the player's stack or

    b.)   Verbally declaring the full amount prior to the initial placement of chips into the pot or

    c.)   Verbally declaring "raise" prior to the placement of the amount to call into the pot and then completing the action with one additional motion back to the player's stack.

83. If a player puts in a raise of 50 percent or more of the previous bet but less than the minimum raise, he or she will be required to make a full raise. The raise will be exactly the minimum raise allowed. A. In no-limit and pot-limit, all raises must be equal to or greater than the size of the previous bet or raise on that betting round. An all-in wager of less than a full raise does not reopen the betting to a player who has already acted. Exception: two consecutive all-in wagers that exceed the minimum allowable bet or raise. By way of example, player A - bets 500, player B - raises to 1,000, player C - calls 1,000, player D - moves all-in for 1,300, player E - moves all-in for 1,700. If player A calls or folds, then players B & C will have an option to raise. The minimum allowable raise will be equal to the last complete raise. In this example, the last complete raise was 500; therefore, players B or C would be allowed to call 1,700 and raise 500 for a total wager of 2,200. (The half-the-size rule for reopening the betting is for limit poker only.)

84. Putting a single oversized chip or multiple same-denomination chips into the pot will be considered a call if the player doesn't announce a raise. For example, a player who places two 500 chips into the pot on a 300-600 blind level when the bet is 600 without an announcement will be considered a call. If a player puts an oversized chip into the pot and says, "Raise," but doesn't state the amount, the raise will be the maximum allowable up to the denomination of that chip. To make a raise with a single oversized chip, a verbal declaration must be made before the chip hits the table surface. After the flop, an initial bet of a single oversized chip without comment will signify a bet equal to the size of the chip.

85. There is no cap on the number of raises in no-limit games. In limit events there will be a maximum of one bet and four raises, even if there are only two players remaining in the hand. Once the Tournament becomes heads-up, this rule does not apply. There may be unlimited raises at the heads-up level.

86. Players are entitled to be informed of the pot size in pot-limit games only. Dealers will not count the pot in limit and no-limit games. If requested, dealers may spread the pot so that it can be counted by a player.

87. Dealers will be responsible for calling string bets/raises. All players at the table are encouraged to assist in calling a string bet/raise if a dealer fails to identify it. String bets/raises called by a player must be verified by a floor person. A string bet/raise is defined as attempting a bet or raise in multiple movements that include a return to a player's stack without a prior verbal declaration of intent or visual deception intended to induce action out of turn before a player's action is complete.

88. Players must keep their highest denomination chips visible at all times.

89. All chips must be visible at all times. Players may not hold or transport Tournament chips in any manner that takes them out of view or out of the Tournament area. A player who does so will forfeit the chips and face disqualification. The forfeited chips will be taken out of play.

90. If a dealer kills an unprotected hand, the player will have no redress and will not be entitled to his or her money back. An exception would be if a player raised and his or her raise had not been called yet, he or she would be entitled to receive his or her raise back.

91. There will be no foreign objects on the table except for a maximum of one card cap. Card caps can be no larger than two (2) inches in diameter and no more than one-half (1/2) inch in depth. Players may not place any food or beverages on the poker table with the exception of one (1) capped bottle of water.

92. In its sole and absolute discretion, Rio may impose penalties ranging from a verbal warning, one missed hand away from the table up to disqualification and expulsion from all Rio casino properties. Penalties will be invoked in cases of soft-play, abuse or disruptive behavior. A penalty will also be imposed if a player throws a card off the table, forcefully mucks their cards causing one or all cards to turn over, violates the one-player-to-a-hand rule or engages in similar behavior.

A. Tournament officials can assess a verbal warning, a missed hand, or one-round, two-round, three-round or four-round penalties and disqualification.

B. A missed-hand penalty will be assessed as follows: The offender can miss one hand or one to four rounds of hands away from the table. The offender's missed hand is counted as part of the round when a penalty is given.

C. Players who receive a missed-hand penalty must remain outside the designated Tournament areas for the length of their penalty.

D. The player must notify the Tournament staff prior to returning to their seat. Repeat infractions are subject to escalating penalties up to disqualification.

E. Rio will maintain a written log of all penalties issued throughout the duration of the WSOP.

F. It should be noted that penalties may not always be imposed in successive manner. Tournament staff in their sole discretion, for example, can disqualify a person for a first offense if action of player is deemed worthy. Or a player, for example, may forego a warning and be assessed a three round penalty. Players should know any conduct deemed penalty-worthy could result in a wide range of discipline for a first offense.

93.   Players are obligated to protect the other players in the tournament at all times. Therefore, whether in a hand or not, players may not

a.)   Disclose contents of live or folded hands,

b.)   Advise or criticize play before the action is completed, or

c.)   Read a hand that hasn't been tabled. While in a hand, players may not a) discuss hands or strategy with any spectator, or b) seek or receive consultation from an outside source. The one-player-to-a-hand rule will be enforced. Players who violate this rule are subject to penalty in accordance with Rules 37, 92, and 96.

94.   A player exposing his or her cards with action pending will incur a penalty, but will not have a dead hand. The penalty will begin at the end of the hand. All players at the table are entitled to see the exposed card(s), if requested.

95.   Poker is an individual game. Soft play will result in penalties that may include forfeiture of chips and/or disqualification. Chip dumping will result in disqualification.

96.   A player who is disqualified shall have his or her chips removed from play and no refund will be provided to that disqualified player. Any player who forfeits play for health or other personal reasons after the start of a Tournament will have his or her chips blinded off accordingly.

97.   Repeated etiquette violations will result in the imposition of penalties assessed by the Tournament Staff. Examples include, but are not limited to, unnecessarily touching other players' cards or chips, delay of the game, repeatedly acting out of turn or excessive chatter.

SECTION VII -TOURNAMENT OPERATIONS POLICIES AND PROCEDURES

98.   There will be dinner Breaks for all events that begin at 12 noon. It will be anticipated to begin after the end of six levels of play. Dinner Breaks will last 90 minutes. There will be no staggered Dinner breaks.

99.   There will be no Dinner Break for events that begin at 5 p.m. An extended break will be awarded after four levels of play and will last 60 minutes. There will be no staggered breaks.

100.   There will be no Dinner Break for any re-started event other than the Main Event Championship, Event #57. Players in re-started events will take an hour-long break at the conclusion of four (4) additional levels of play.

101.   Play will end after 10 levels of play for all events that begin at 12 noon. Play will resume the following day at 2:30 p.m. The Tournament Director may modify this schedule for any reason.

102.   Play will end after eight levels of play for all events that begin at 5 p.m. Play will resume the following day at 3 p.m. The Tournament Director may modify this schedule for any reason.

103.   Play on Day 2 will be suspended at 3 a.m., and will resume the following day at 3 p.m. If an event is running long, play may be suspended on subsequent days at the discretion of the Tournament Director.

104.   Ten minutes prior to the end of days play for any event, a random card will be drawn to determine how many additional hands will be played. Playing Cards 3-7 will be used and a random player will be asked to pick a card face down.

105.   Upon nearing the "Money" (the first level of the prize pool payout), a "Hand-for-Hand" method of determining player placement within the prize pool and the actual amount of prize pool disbursement within that event will be utilized. This will begin by completing the current hand in progress at all tables. Once all hands are complete, the dealer at each table will deal one hand only, then – once the hand is complete – suspend play. This process will continue until enough players have been eliminated to reach the money. During the Hand-for-Hand process, more than one player may be eliminated during the same hand. If two players are eliminated during the same hand at different tables, both players will "tie" for that place finish. If two players are eliminated during the same hand at the same table, the player who began that hand with the highest chip count will receive the higher place finish.

WORLD SERIES OF POKER QUIZ

By Dana Smith

How much do you know about the world's premier gaming event? Test your knowledge with these 10 brainteasers taken from "The Championship Table at the World Series of Poker."

QUESTIONS

1. What was the first year that more than 100 players entered the WSOP Main Event?
2. In addition to Johnny Moss, who are the three men who have won the championship title two years in a row?
3. What was the shortest-lived event in WSOP history?
4. When was the first ladies championship tournament held?
5. What was the first year the WSOP championship event was video taped?
6. Who is the only woman ever to make it to the final table of the WSOP championship event?
7. Who has made it to the final table of the championship event the most times?
8. Who was the youngest player ever to win the WSOP championship event?

9. Which card rank has appeared in the winning hand more often than any other?

10. Which card has appeared most often in the losing hand?

ANSWERS

1. In 1982 there were 102 entries, up from 75 in 1981. In 2003 there were 839. In 2006 there were 8,773!

2. Doyle Brunson, 1976-77; Stu Ungar, 1980-81; Johnny Chan, 1987-88

3. Chinese Poker, 1995-1996

4. 1977. Jackie McDaniels won $5,580.

5. 1973. Puggy Pearson won it. Jimmy "The Greek" Snyder narrated it.

6. Barbara Enright finished in fifth place in 1995. She won $114,180.

7. It's a toss-up between Johnny Moss & Doyle Brunson, about 8 times each.

8. Joe Cada was 21 years old when he won in 2009.

9. Surprisingly, the winner was holding a nine in his hand at 8 championship tables.

10. Even more surprising, the loser was holding an ace at 12 championship tables.

GLOSSARY

ace-to-five:
A variation of low poker in which the best and lowest card is the ace, straights and flushes don't count, and the best hand is A-2-3-4-5. Compare with DEUCE-TO-SEVEN.

act:
To bet, raise, fold, or check.

all in:
When a player has all his chips committed to a pot.

ante:
1. Mandatory bet placed into the pot by all players before the cards are dealt; compare with BLIND. 2. Put such a bet in the pot.

backdoor:
Make an unlikely straight or flush late in a hand by catching successive cards on the last rounds of play.

before the flop:
See PREFLOP.

bet:
A wager; often specifically the chips or money placed in a pot.

bicycle:
See WHEEL.

big blind:

1. The larger of two FORCED BLIND bets in flop games such as hold'em and Omaha, posted before the cards are dealt by the player two seats to the left of the BUTTON. Compare to SMALL BLIND. 2. The player occupying this position.

big slick:

In hold'em, hole cards of A-K.

blind:

1. A mandatory bet made before the cards are dealt by the player or players immediately to the button's left. 2. The player making that bet.

bluff:

1. Bet aggressively with an inferior hand, one unlikely to win if called, to cause opponents to fold better hands, thus making the bluffer a winner by default. 2. A bet so made.

board:

1. The COMMUNITY CARDS in FLOP GAMES. 2. A player's upcards in stud games.

bracelet:

The gold bracelet given to the winner of a World Series of Poker event. Also, *gold bracelet.*

bring-in (bet):

1. A forced bet that the holder of the high or low card, depending on the variation, must make on the first round of play in seven-card stud and some other variations. 2. The amount required to open betting.

bubble:

In a tournament, the point at which all remaining players will win money except for the next player to get eliminated. For example, with 37 players remaining and 36 places paid, that 37th place is the *bubble.*

button:

1. The player occupying the dealer position who, in games with BLINDS, goes last in all rounds except the first. 2. The physical disk, often plastic and labeled "dealer," that indicates the dealer position.

buy-In:

A player's investment of cash to gain entry into a poker tournament (or a cash game).

call:

Match a bet on the current round of betting and stay in competition for the pot, as opposed to FOLD or RAISE.

cash:

Be among the top finishers in a tournament and win a cash prize.

check:

The act of "not betting" and passing the bet option to the next player while still remaining an active player. Once a bet has been made in a round, checking is not an option.

check-raise:

Raise in a round after first checking, essentially trapping a player.

chip leader:

In a tournament, the player with the most chips.

coin flip:

A hand or situation whose winning chances approximate 50-50; one in which neither side has a great advantage over the other. For example, in hold'em, A-K versus two queens.

community cards:

In hold'em and Omaha, the cards dealt to the center of the table that are shared by all players. Also, *board*.

cowboys:

Kings.

dead money:

1. Disparaging term for a player who has little chance of winning. 2. Money put into the pot by players who have folded and are no longer in competition for it.

deal:

1. The act of distributing cards to the players. 2. In a tournament, an agreement between players at a final table to divide a certain portion of the prize money before the final outcome.

dealer:

The person who shuffles the cards and deals them to all the players. In a WSOP tournament, the dealer is a house employee and not a participant in the game and has the responsibility of running the game smoothly.

defend the blind:

In the small or big blind position, call a raise made by an opponent in middle to late position who is suspected of raising to force out opponents.

deuce-to-seven:

Low poker in which the lowest and best card is a deuce and the highest, and therefore worst, is an ace. Flushes and straights count against the player, so the best hand is 2-3-4-5-7 of mixed suits. Also called *Kansas City lowball.* Compare with ACE-TO-FIVE.

donkey:

An unskilled and perpetually losing poker player.

double-suited:

A hand that has possibilities of making a flush in either of two suits; usually refers to a starting Omaha hand with two cards each of two suits.

double up:
> Double one's bankroll on a single hand by being all-in against another player and winning the showdown. Also, *double through.*

downcard:
> A card that can be viewed only by the player holding it; HOLE CARD. Any card that is not exposed to players.

draw:
> The exchange of cards allowed after the first round of betting in draw poker variations.

draw dead:
> Have a hand with more cards to come that is hopelessly beat, no matter what cards are dealt.

drawing hand:
> A hand that needs improvement to form some strength, usually referring to an unmade straight or flush.

early position:
> Approximately the first third of players to act in a nine- or 10-handed game or the first or second to act in a six- or seven-handed game.

8-or-better:
> In HI-LOW, a requirement that a player must have a card no higher than an 8 and no cards paired for his five-card hand to qualify for the low end of the pot.

face down:
> A card positioned such that its rank and suit faces the table and cannot be viewed. A DOWNCARD or HOLE CARD.

face up:
> A card positioned such that its rank and suit faces up and is therefore visible to all players. Cards dealt this way are also known as *Upcards* or *Open Cards.*

fifth street:

1. In seven-card stud, the fifth card dealt to players along with the betting round accompanying it. 2. In hold'em and Omaha, the final round of betting, named for the fifth COMMUNITY CARD dealt; more commonly called the RIVER.

final table:

In a tournament, the final table of players, which comes with prestige and big money.

flop:

In hold'em and Omaha, the three COMMUNITY CARDS that are simultaneously dealt face up upon completion of the first round of betting and can be used by all active players.

flush:

A poker hand consisting of five cards of the same suit, such as Q♠ 9♠ 8♠ 5♠ 2♠, a queen-high spade flush.

fold:

Get rid of one's cards, thereby becoming inactive in the current hand and ineligible to play for the pot.

four-card flush:

A hand containing four cards of the same suit.

four-card straight:

A hand containing four cards in sequence, such as 2-3-4-5, needing one more to complete the straight.

four of a kind:

A poker hand containing four cards of the same rank. Also, *quads*.

fourth street:

1. In seven-card stud, the fourth card dealt to players, along with the betting round accompanying it. 2. In hold'em and Omaha, the third round of betting, named for the fourth COMMUNITY CARD dealt; more commonly called the TURN.

freeze-out:

A tournament or game played until one player has all the chips.

full house:

A poker hand consisting of three of a kind and a pair, such as 7-7-7-K-K, called a *full house of sevens over kings* or *sevens full of kings*. Also *full boat* or simply, *full*.

gap:

The missing card in an INSIDE STRAIGHT draw, for example, 6-7-9-10 for which an 8 is needed to make a straight.

go all in:

Bet all one's chips.

gold bracelet:

See BRACELET.

gutshot:

See INSIDE STRAIGHT.

hand for hand:

The situation that arises when players are on the BUBBLE in a tournament and all dealers are instructed to wait after completion of their hands before another round of cards is dealt so that each table will play one hand at a time until a player busts out.

heads-up:

Poker played by two players only, one against the other. 2. A pot contested by two players. Also, *head-to-head*.

high card:

The poker hand that has no higher-ranking combinations, such as a pair, two pair, or better; basically five odd cards. Such a hand is named by its highest-ranking card.

hi-low:

Poker variation in which players compete for the best high and low hands, with the winner of each getting half the pot.

If one hand is both the best high and the best low, that hand wins the entire pot. Also called *hi-low split*.

hi-low split:

HI-LOW.

hold'em:

A high poker game featuring two starting down cards, a FLOP of three shared COMMUNITY CARDS, a fourth community card (the TURN), and then a fifth (the RIVER), with four betting rounds. At the showdown, any combination of the best five out of the seven available cards wins the pot. The "official" name of the game is *Texas hold'em*.

hole card:

A card held face down by a player, the value of which is hidden from other players. Also, DOWNCARD, *pocket card*.

H.O.R.S.E.:

A game with rounds rotating among five variations, limit hold'em, Omaha 8-or-better, razz, seven-card stud high, and seven-card stud 8-or-better. Typically each variation lasts for one round of cards; sometimes, for a specified time limit.

inside straight:

1. A STRAIGHT draw consisting of four cards with one "hole," such that only one rank can complete the hand, for example, 2-4-5-6, in which only a 3 can complete the straight. Also, *gutshot*. Compare to an OPEN-ENDED STRAIGHT which has two ranks (eight OUTS) to complete.

in the money:

In a tournament, to finish among the top players and win cash.

lammer:

A chip usually received as a result of winning a satellite-type tournament, which can be used to buy into bigger tournament events, or often, turned into cash.

late position:
> The last two or three seats in a nine- or 10-handed game, or the last or next-to-last player in a game with five to seven players.

level:
> ROUND, definition 1.

limit:
> A shortening of LIMIT POKER.

limit poker:
> The type of betting structure for poker games in which the minimum and maximum bet sizes are set at fixed amounts, for example, a $5/$10 game, in which bets or raises are all in increments of $5 in early specified betting rounds and in increments of $10 in later specified betting rounds. Compare with POT LIMIT and NO LIMIT.

limp:
> Call a bet, that is, not raise, as a way to enter the pot cheaply, or, if the first player to make a bet, open for the minimum. Also, *limp in*.

loose:
> 1. A player who plays many hands and enters many pots. 2. When applied to a game, a collection of players who play many pots.

Main Event:
> The $10,000 buy-in final event at the WSOP which crowns the annual world poker champion.

main pot:
> When a player is ALL IN and two or more competing players still have chips, the original pot containing the matched bets and raises of all players, as opposed to SIDE POT, a segregated pot created for the players who still have chips to wager.

megasatellite:

A lower buy-in tournament featuring multiple tables and no rebuys, in which the top finishers win lammers, chips which can be used to buy in to tournaments for a fraction of the cost, or traded in for cash.

misdeal:

A deal deemed illegal and therefore invalid.

mixed games:

A new WSOP event featuring eight different styles of poker: deuce-to-seven triple draw lowball, limit hold'em, Omaha hi-low 8-or-better, razz, seven-card stud (high), pot-limit high, seven-card stud hi-low 8-or-better, and no-limit hold'em.

money management:

A strategy used by smart players to preserve their capital, manage their wins, and avoid unnecessary risks and big losses.

monster:

A very big poker hand.

muck:

1. Fold. 2. The area on the table where discarded cards are placed.

no-limit:

Betting structure in which the maximum bet allowed is limited only by the amount of chips the bettor has on the table.

nut flush:

The best flush possible, given the cards on board.

offsuit:

Cards of different suits. Also, *unsuited.*

Omaha:

1. A high poker game featuring four starting downcards, a FLOP of three shared COMMUNITY CARDS, a fourth community card (the TURN), and then a fifth (the RIVER),

with four betting rounds. At the showdown, the final hand must consist of two cards from the player's hand—no more, no less—and three cards from the board (as opposed to HOLD'EM in which any five cards can be used). The best five-card hand wins the pot. Can be played high or hi-low. 2. Specifically, the high-only version of the game—sometimes called *Omaha high*.

Omaha high:
OMAHA played high only.

Omaha hi-low 8-or-better:
OMAHA played HI-LOW with a requirement that the best low hand must have five unpaired cards of 8 or lower to win the low half of the pot or else the best high hand will win the entire pot.

one pair:
A poker hand containing two cards of the same rank, such as Q-Q or 7-7.

on tilt:
A player who has lost control of his emotions due to a bad loss or succession of losses and is playing recklessly. Also, *steaming*.

open-ended straight:
Four consecutive cards to a STRAIGHT (not including an ace, which would make it a ONE-ENDED STRAIGHT) such as 8-9-10-J, such that a card on either end will make a straight, as opposed to an INSIDE STRAIGHT.

outs:
Cards that will improve a hand that is behind enough to win a pot.

overcard:
A HOLE CARD higher in rank than any board card. For example, if a player holds A-10 and the flop is K-J-6, the ace is an overcard.

oversized chip:

A chip, put into a pot, of greater value than what is required. For example, a player puts a $100 chip in for a $50 blind or a $1,000 chip when it is his turn to call a $100 bet. Also, *overchip*.

pocket cards:

The initial cards a player is dealt; in hold'em (two cards) and Omaha (four cards). In stud games, the face down cards held individually by each player. Also HOLE CARDS.

pocket rockets:

Pocket aces.

position:

1. A player's relative order of acting compared to opponents, particularly with respect to the number of players acting after his turn. 2. Specifically good position, that is later and better than opponents.

pot:

The total of all bets placed in the center of the table by players during a poker hand and collected by the winner or winners of that hand.

pot-limit:

A betting structure in which the maximum bet allowed is limited by the current size of the pot. For example, if the pot is $25, a player may bet $25, and the next player can either call the $25 bet, raise it $50 (the minimum raise), or raise $75 (the size of the pot including his $25 call).

pot odds:

The amount of money in the pot compared to the cost of a bet. For example if $50 is in the pot, and a player needs to call a bet of $10 to play, he is getting pot odds of 5 to 1.

preflop:
> In hold'em, Omaha, and other flop variations, the action that occurs after players receive their starting cards and before the three-card FLOP is dealt.

premium hand:
> One in a group of the best starting hands in a poker game.

protect a hand:
> 1. Carefully cover one's cards when looking so that opponents cannot read their values. 2. Place a chip or small token over one's cards so that the dealer doesn't mistakenly remove them. 3. Bet or raise with a hand so that opponents have to pay a steep price to go for a lucky draw.

quads:
> FOUR OF A KIND.

quartered:
> In a HI-LOW game, having split either the low or high end of a pot such that only one-fourth of the chips are won.

race off:
> In a tournament, when all the smaller denomination chips are changed to the next highest denomination so that the smaller chips will no longer be in play, with the odd leftover chips, colored-up and awarded to players dealt the highest cards, with a one chip per player maximum.

raise:
> 1. A wager that increases the size of a current bet such that opponents, including the original bettor, must put additional money into the pot to stay active in a hand. 2. The actual chips or money that constitute this action.

razz:
> Seven-card stud played for low.

reraise:
> Raise a raise, that is, call an opponent's increased bet and commit even more chips to the pot.

river:
> 1. In hold'em and Omaha, the fifth and last community card dealt or its betting round (or both considered together). 2. In stud games, the last card each player receives or its betting round (or both considered together).

rough:
> A lowball hand with relatively weak supporting cards, for example, 8-7-6-5-3 is a *rough 8,* as opposed to a *smooth 8,* such as 8-5-3-2-A.

round:
> 1. In a tournament, a fixed period of play that ends with increased blinds or antes or both. Also *level.* 2. The complete cycle of checks, bets, folds, and raises occurring after each new card or cards are dealt.

royal flush:
> The poker hand consisting of 10-J-Q-K-A of the same suit, the highest-ranking hand in standard poker without wild cards.

satellite:
> At the WSOP, a one-table tournament in which the winner gains the cash equivalent value for a larger-buy-in tournament at a fraction of the cost.

scoop:
> In a HI-LOW game, win both the high and low ends of a pot.

semibluff:
> Bet or raise with a hand that is perceived to be second-best or worse but has two ways to win, either by forcing opponents out, or if that fails, by improving to a winner with a fortuitous draw.

set:
> A three-of-a-kind hand made with a pair in the hole and one on board..

seven-card stud:

A poker variation in which players start with two downcards and an upcard along with a betting round, then receive three more up cards and a final down card, with a betting round after each card dealt, for a total of five betting rounds. At the end, the best five-card hand wins.

seven-card stud 8-or-better:

SEVEN-CARD STUD played HI-LOW featuring three starting cards, two down and one up, then three successive rounds of upcards with a final seventh card dealt face down for a total of five betting rounds. To qualify for low, a player has to have five unpaired cards of 8 or less or the best high hand will win the entire pot.

seventh street:

In seven-card stud, the seventh and last card received along with the betting round accompanying it. Also, *river.*

shootout tournament:

A multiple-table tournament in which each table is played down to one winner, who then moves on to the next round, until only one player is left, the champion.

short-handed:

A game played with less than the full or typical number of players. In hold'em, a game played with six or fewer players.

short stack:

A player who has relatively few chips in comparison to opponents or the blinds.

showdown:

The final act of a poker hand, the point at which remaining players reveal their hands to determine the winner of the pot.

show one, show all:

A rule requiring a player to show all opponents his cards if he shows any one player.

"shuffle up and deal":

The traditional opening words to WSOP tournaments.

side pot:

When one player has bet all his chips and two or more opponents remain, a segregated pot created for and that can only be won by players who still have chips to bet, as opposed to the MAIN POT, the collection of original bets by all active players.

sixth street:

In seven-card stud, the sixth card received along with the betting round accompanying it.

small blind:

1. The smaller of two forced BLIND bets in hold'em and Omaha, posted before the cards are dealt by the player immediately to the left of the BUTTON. Compare to BIG BLIND. 2. The player occupying this position.

smooth:

A lowball hand with relatively strong supporting cards, for example, 8-5-3-2-A is a smooth 8, as opposed to a rough 8, such as 8-7-6-3-2.

splash the pot:

Bet chips so that some or all land and commingle with chips already in the pot, causing it to be unclear how much was actually wagered—disallowed in tournaments.

split pot:

When two or more players are tied for the best hand and divide the pot evenly.

steal the blinds:

On the first round of betting, bluff opponents out of a pot no one has entered so that the blinds (and antes, if any) can be won without a fight.

straight:

A poker hand consisting of five consecutive cards of mixed suits, such as 4-5-6-7-8 or 10-J-Q-K-A. A straight may not "wrap" around the ace, so Q-K-A-2-3 is not a straight, but merely an ace-high hand.

straight draw:
> Three or four cards to a possible straight, such as 4-5-7 or 8-9-10-J.

straight flush:
> A poker hand consisting of five consecutive cards in the same suit, such as 7♠ 8♠ 9♠ 10♠ J♠, called a *jack-high straight flush*. A straight-flush may not wrap around the ace, thus K⋯ A⋯ 2⋯ 3⋯ 4⋯ is not a straight-flush, but an ace-high diamond flush.

string bet:
> Additional chips added to a bet that has already been placed, that is, a player's hand has been removed from the chips wagered, making such bet official and final (unless declared otherwise verbally). String bets are disallowed at the WSOP.

suited connectors:
> Cards that are of consecutive rank and in the same suit, such as 8♠ 9♠.

tell:
> An inadvertent mannerism or reaction that reveals information about the strength of a player's hand.

Texas hold'em:
> HOLD'EM.

three of a kind:
> A poker hand containing three cards of the same rank, such as 4-4-4, called *three fours*. Also *trips*.

tight:
> A player who plays only premium hands and enters few pots.

tournament:
> At the WSOP, a competition among players who start with an equal number of chips and play until one player holds all the chips. Players compete for cash and get eliminated when they run out of chips.

tournament director:
The supervisor responsible for handling disputes, and organizing and running a tournament.

triple draw:
Five card draw LOWBALL with three separate draws in which players get to replace unwanted cards with new ones, and with four rounds of betting (as opposed to the two in traditional draw poker). Triple draw is often played DEUCE-TO-SEVEN.

turn:
The fourth community card in flop games such as Omaha and Texas hold'em. Also *fourth street*.

two pair:
A poker hand containing two sets of two cards of the same rank, such as A-A-5-5, called *aces and fives*.

underdog:
1. A hand or situation that is likely to lose or perceived to be likely to lose. Also, *dog*.

upcard:
A card that can be viewed by all players.

wheel:
1. In low poker, the best hand possible; in ACE-TO-FIVE, A-2-3-4-5; in DEUCE-TO-SEVEN, 2-3-4-5-7 that is not a flush.

World Championship of Poker:
The $10,000-buy-in no-limit hold'em Main Event at the WORLD SERIES OF POKER, acknowledged as the official and accepted world championship.

World Series of Poker:
The World Championship of Poker events that are held every year.

WSOP:
World Series of Poker.

GREAT CARDOZA POKER BOOKS
ADD THESE TO YOUR LIBRARY - ORDER NOW!

THE POKER TOURNAMENT FORMULA *by Arnold Snyder.* Start making money now in fast no-limit hold'em tournaments with these radical and never-before-published concepts and secrets for beating tournaments. You'll learn why cards don't matter as much as the dynamics of a tournament—your position, the size of your chip stack, who your opponents are, and above all, the structure. Poker tournaments offer one of the richest opportunities to come along in decades. Every so often, a book comes along that changes the way players attack a game and provides them with a big advantage over opponents. Gambling legend Arnold Snyder has written such a book. 368 pages, $19.95.

POKER TOURNAMENT FORMULA 2: Advanced Strategies for Big Money Tournaments *by Arnold Snyder.* Probably the greatest tournament poker book ever written, and the most controversial in the last decade, Snyder's revolutionary work debunks commonly (and falsely) held beliefs. Snyder reveals the power of chip utility—the real secret behind winning tournaments—and covers utility ranks, tournament structures, small- and long-ball strategies, patience factors, the impact of structures, crushing the Harringbots and other player types, tournament phases, and much more. Includes big sections on Tools, Strategies, and Tournament Phases. A must buy! 496 pages, $24.95.

HOW TO BEAT SIT-AND-GO POKER TOURNAMENTS by Neil Timothy. There is a lot of dead money up for grabs in the lower limit sit-and-gos and Neil Timothy shows you how to go and get it. The author, a professional player, shows you how to reach the last six places of lower limit sit-and-go tournaments four out of five times and then how to get in the money 25-35 percent of the time using his powerful, proven strategies. This book can turn a losing sit-and-go player into a winner, and a winner into a bigger winner. Also effective for the early and middle stages of one-table satellites.176 pages, $14.95.

DANIEL NEGREANU'S POWER HOLD'EM STRATEGY *by Daniel Negreanu.* This power-packed book on beating no-limit hold'em is one of the three most influential poker books ever written. Negreanu headlines a collection of young great players—Todd Brunson, David Williams. Erick Lindgren, Evelyn Ng and Paul Wasicka—who share their insider professional moves and winning secrets. You'll learn about short-handed and heads-up play, high-limit cash games, a powerful beginner's strategy to neutralize pro players, and how to mix up your play, bluff and win big pots. The centerpiece, however, is Negreanu's powerful and revolutionary small ball strategy. You'll learn how to play hold'em with cards you never would have played before—and with fantastic results. The preflop, flop, turn and river will never look the same again. A must-have! 520 pages, $34.95.

POKER WIZARDS *by Warwick Dunnett.* In the tradition of Super System, an exclusive collection of champions and superstars have been brought together to share their strategies, insights, and tactics for winning big money at poker, specifically no-limit hold'em tournaments. This is priceless advice from players who individually have each made millions of dollars in tournaments, and collectively, have won more than 20 WSOP bracelets, two WSOP main events, 100 major tournaments and $50 million in tournament winnings! Featuring Daniel Negreanu, Dan Harrington, Marcel Luske, Kathy Liebert, Mike Sexton, Mel Judah, Marc Salem, T.J Cloutier and Chris "Jesus" Ferguson. This must-read book is a goldmine for serious players, aspiring pros, and future champions! 352 pgs, $19.95.

HOLD'EM WISDOM FOR ALL PLAYERS *by Daniel Negreanu.* Superstar poker player Daniel Negreanu provides 50 easy-to-read and right-to-the-point hold'em strategy nuggets that will immediately make you a better player at cash games and tournaments. His wit and wisdom makes for great reading; even better, it makes for killer winning advice. Conversational, straightforward, and educational, this book covers topics as diverse as the top 10 rookie mistakes to bullying bullies and exploiting your table image. 176 pages, $14.95.

GREAT CARDOZA POKER BOOKS
ADD THESE TO YOUR LIBRARY - ORDER NOW!

SUPER SYSTEM *by Doyle Brunson.* This classic book is considered by the pros to be the best book ever written on poker! Jam-packed with advanced strategies, theories, tactics and money-making techniques, no serious poker player can afford to be without this hard-hitting information. Includes fifty pages of the most precise poker statistics ever published. Features chapters written by poker's biggest superstars, such as Dave Sklansky, Mike Caro, Chip Reese, Joey Hawthorne, Bobby Baldwin, and Doyle. Essential strategies, advanced play, and no-nonsense winning advice on making money at 7-card stud (razz, high-low split, cards speak, and declare), draw poker, lowball, and hold'em (limit and no-limit).This is a must-read for any serious poker player. 628 pages, $29.95.

SUPER SYSTEM 2 *by Doyle Brunson.* SS2 expands upon the original with more games and professional secrets from the best in the world. Revision includes Phil Hellmuth along with superstars Daniel Negreanu, winner of four WSOP bracelets and 2004 Poker Player of the Year; Lyle Berman, 3-time WSOP bracelet winner, founder of the World Poker Tour, and super-high stakes cash player; Bobby Baldwin, 1978 World Champion; Johnny Chan, 2-time World Champion and 10-time WSOP bracelet winner; Mike Caro, poker's greatest theorist and instructor; Jennifer Harman, the world's top female player; Todd Brunson, winner of more than 20 tournaments; and Crandell Addington, no-limit legend. 704 pgs, $29.95.

THE GODFATHER OF POKER *by Doyle Brunson.* Doyle Brunson's riveting autobiography is a story of guts and glory, of good luck and bad, of triumph and unspeakable tragedy. It is a story of beating the odds, of a man who bet $1 million on a hole of golf—when he could barely stand! Here is a man whose most outrageous bluff came with a gunman pointing a pistol at his forehead. He has survived whippings, gun fights, mobsters, killers and a bout with cancer where the doctor told him his hand was played out. Apparently, fate had never played poker with Brunson; he lived. Doyle has searched for Noah's ark, tried to raise the Titanic, won two poker championships, and lived a life of gusto. 352 pages, $26.95

CHAMPIONSHIP NO-LIMIT & POT-LIMIT HOLD'EM *by T. J. Cloutier & Tom McEvoy.* New edition! The bible for winning pot-limit and no-limit hold'em gives you the answers to your most important questions: How do you get inside your opponents' heads and learn how to beat them at their own game? How can you tell how much to bet, raise, and reraise in no-limit hold'em? When can you bluff? How do you set up your opponents in pot-limit hold'em so that you can win a monster pot? What are the best strategies for winning no-limit and pot-limit tournaments, satellites, and supersatellites? Rock-solid and inspired advice you can bank on from two of the most recognizable figures in poker. 304 pages, $19.95.

CHAMPIONSHIP OMAHA (Omaha High-Low, Pot-limit Omaha, Limit High Omaha) *by Tom McEvoy & T.J. Cloutier.* New edition! Clearly-written strategies and powerful advice from Cloutier and McEvoy who have won four World Series of Poker Omaha titles. You'll learn how to beat low-limit and high-stakes games, play against loose and tight opponents, and the differing strategies for rebuy and freezeout tournaments. Learn the best starting hands, when slowplaying a big hand is dangerous, what danglers are (and why winners don't play them), why you sometimes fold the nuts on the flop and would be correct in doing so, and overall, how you can win a lot of money at Omaha! 272 pages, illustrations, $19.95.

CARO'S BOOK OF POKER TELLS *by Mike Caro.* One of the ten greatest books written on poker, this must-have book should be in every player's library. If you're serious about winning, you'll realize that most of the profit comes from being able to read your opponents. Caro reveals the secrets of interpreting *tells*—physical reactions that reveal information about a player's cards—such as shrugs, sighs, shaky hands, eye contact, and many more. Learn when opponents are bluffing, when they aren't and why—based solely on their mannerisms. Over 170 photos of players in action and play-by-play examples show the actual tells. These powerful ideas will give you the decisive edge. 320 pages, $24.95.

POWERFUL WINNING POKER SIMULATIONS
A MUST FOR SERIOUS PLAYERS WITH A COMPUTER!
IBM compatible CD ROM Win 95, 98, 2000, NT, ME, XP

These incredible full color poker simulations are the best method to improve your game. Computer opponents play like real players. All games let you set the limits and rake and have fully programmable players, plus stat tracking, and Hand Analyzer for starting hands. Mike Caro, the world's foremost poker theoretician says, "Amazing... a steal for under $500... get it, it's great." Includes free phone support. "Smart Advisor" gives expert advice for every play!

1. TURBO TEXAS HOLD'EM FOR WINDOWS - $59.95. Choose which players, and how many (2-10) you want to play, create loose/tight games, and control check-raising, bluffing, position, sensitivity to pot odds, and more! Also, instant replay, pop-up odds, Professional Advisor keeps track of play statistics. Free bonus: Hold'em Hand Analyzer analyzes all 169 pocket hands in detail and their win rates under any conditions you set. Caro says this "hold'em software is the most powerful ever created." Great product!

2. TURBO SEVEN-CARD STUD FOR WINDOWS - $59.95. Create any conditions of play; choose number of players (2-8), bet amounts, fixed or spread limit, bring-in method, tight/loose conditions, position, reaction to board, number of dead cards, and stack deck to create special conditions. Features instant replay. Terrific stat reporting includes analysis of starting cards, 3-D bar charts, and graphs. Play interactively and run high speed simulation to test strategies. Hand Analyzer analyzes starting hands in detail. Wow!

3. TURBO OMAHA HIGH-LOW SPLIT FOR WINDOWS - $59.95. Specify any playing conditions; betting limits, number of raises, blind structures, button position, aggressiveness/passiveness of opponents, number of players (2-10), types of hands dealt, blinds, position, board reaction, and specify flop, turn, and river cards! Choose opponents and use provided point count or create your own. Statistical reporting, instant replay, pop-up odds high speed simulation to test strategies, amazing Hand Analyzer, and much more!

4. TURBO OMAHA HIGH FOR WINDOWS - $59.95. Same features as above, but tailored for Omaha High only. Caro says program is "an electrifying research tool...it can clearly be worth thousands of dollars to any serious player. A must for Omaha High players.

5. TURBO 7 STUD 8 OR BETTER - $59.95. Brand new with all the features you expect from the Wilson Turbo products: the latest artificial intelligence, instant advice and exact odds, play versus 2-7 opponents, enhanced data charts that can be exported or printed, the ability to fold out of turn and immediately go to the next hand, ability to peek at opponents hand, optional warning mode that warns you if a play disagrees with the advisor, and automatic mode that runs up to 50 tests unattended. Tough computer players vary their styles for a great game.

6. TOURNAMENT TEXAS HOLD'EM - $39.95

Set-up for tournament practice and play, this realistic simulation pits you against celebrity look-alikes. Tons of options let you control tournament size with 10 to 300 entrants, select limits, ante, rake, blind structures, freezeouts, number of rebuys and competition level of opponents. Pop-up status report shows how you're doing vs. the competition. Save tournaments in progress to play again later. Additional feature allows quick folds on finished hands.

Order now at 1-800-577-WINS or go online to: www.cardozabooks.com